How to Raise a Smart Ass

By Lucia Walinchus

Copyright 2016

Published by Pronoun Books

Prologue

The other day I walked past the front door of my house and discovered it was slightly ajar. This was surprising because, even though Oklahoma is known for its fierce wind, it's a fairly heavy door and it can usually withstand even the strongest barrage.

As I stood there puzzling, it occurred to me that closing the front door would make a noise ... so perhaps it was *left* open on purpose.

I called for my daughter Chloe to ask her about it, but no one responded. That morning I had told her she would have to clean her room if she wanted to go to a friend's house, so I went up to her room — and of course it was empty. At the tender age of 5, Chloe had snuck out of the house. This should make the teenage years quite interesting.

My oldest, Cleopatra, or "Chloe," is now a spunky 6-year-old brunette. She loves playing princesses, reading Dr. Seuss and being a smart aleck.

"I WANT A SNACK! I WANT

BREAD AND BUTTER!" she wailed once as she trailed me into the kitchen, where I was trying to start dinner.

"No, you can't have bread and butter or you'll never eat dinner," I said. "How about carrots?"

"I want a sandwich."

"Alright, whatever, you can have a sandwich for dinner then. Do you want turkey or ham?"

"No, I want a butter sandwich."

"You think you're pretty clever, huh?"

Concetta (Con-chet-ta) is my feisty little blondie, soon to be 4. She enjoys pandas, trolling the house for sharp objects and trying to call people on her phone, which might actually just be a calculator. When she grows up, she wants to be the boss.

"I have feet on," she told me the other day.

"Well, no," I said. "You have bare feet."

"I don't have bear feet!"

"No your feet ARE bare. It's a different kind of bare."

"I AM NOT A BEAR. My name is Chetta!"

Tiny T3 is our son, who is as yet unnamed because it's much more fun to refer to your children as Terminators. Also, he hasn't been born yet, and as the third child is frankly luckily that we've gotten around to assembling the crib. Choosing a name would be much more effort, even without taking the time to locate a hex wrench, which was a job in itself.

I would like to apologize to the world and state that, despite my best efforts to shape the next generation of children into superheroes of society, I discovered that I have missed the mark almost entirely and instead created tiny versions of myself. That is, a smartass. But I am heartened that my reproductive foibles tend to be, at the very least, entertaining. My hope is this book will make you laugh, will make you cry or, at a minimum, you'll buy lots of sanitizer. Kids are messy.

The other day, Chloe got in really close to my face and huffed as hard as she could.

"Hey!" I said, frustrated. "What are you doing?"

She looked back at me and smiled.

"I'm blowing your mind," she said.

Part 1: Southern California & Pennsylvania

Chapter 1: She Who Pees Her Pants and the Night of Nurse Ninja

Ah, the joy of pregnancy! You've created life!

And then there is the realization that you will be able to, for once in your life, go out in fat pants and rock that ba-dunk-a-dunk in your trunk.

"Ha ha!" I bragged to friends at New Year's. "My resolution is to GAIN twenty pounds. Suckers!"

That joy quickly turned to agony as I realized that to gain weight I would probably have to keep food down at some point.

At about two months pregnant, I went to the DMV and waited in line to get a ticket. Because California has a wonderful system whereby you spend an hour waiting outside to get a *number* to then wait *another* hour or so (if you're lucky) for that number to be called.

After about a half-hour in line, because the DMV wasn't painful enough, all of a sudden I started feeling extra hot and knew that this was not going to end well. I couldn't go inside to go to the bathroom because I was afraid that the throng of angry people would think I was cutting in front of them. Not knowing what to do, and starting to feel much, much more nauseated, I ran from the line and threw up in some bushes in front of the office.

After that, the nice people behind me in line were gracious enough to save my spot. They had kids and totally understood how tough it was to be pregnant. Either that, or they thought I had a communicable disease and were much more willing for me to stand in the shade, away from them, than have me breathing out germs in their general vicinity. But I was grateful nonetheless.

Over time, the throwing up got worse and worse until I could barely keep anything down and was pretty much eating a diet of crackers, cheese and prenatal vitamins. Then one night I found

I couldn't even keep that down. I was throwing up nonstop and was pretty much in a ball on my couch.

"I took some Pepto Bismol," I said, after finally reaching a doctor on the phone. "But it still won't stop."

"Oh, honey," the doctor said, "Pepto Bismol is for throwing up on like a level two. What you have is level 10. You have to go to the hospital."

It was a Saturday, but it was Hubby's duty day in the Navy. So with him stuck on a boat, I had a good friend, Karen, take me to the hospital.

We arrived there, tiny trash can in hand to use at appropriate moments. I explained to the desk attendant my dire situation: not being able to stop throwing up, calling the doctor, etc.

"Oh," he said, nonchalant. "You're pregnant." This was clearly not the first time he had heard this. He casually searched around for what felt like ages before finding a pill for me to chew on. I sat back down and waited another two hours, bucket in hand, while everyone around me, it seemed, got called.

Finally, we got back to the doctor and he did an ultrasound to see if the baby was okay. And there she was, dancing the funky chicken.

I guess when you see pictures of babies in the womb, they always look so quiet and peaceful, a slice of serenity floating along in an amniotic sea. But, instead, I saw my little crab directing an underwater orchestra.

"Oh, wow, the baby's really moving around in there," Karen said.

"I know!" I said, entranced by the fetal disco. "Wow."

I originally grew up in the Philadelphia area (Go Flyers!) and went to college in Washington, D.C., where I studied journalism. I met Hubby one night my junior year on the Metro. (He was visiting some mutual friends. I don't randomly pick up strangers on the train. But you can think about that the next time you take public transportation.)

As an officer in the Navy, he was first stationed Charleston, South Carolina, where I worked as a reporter. Charleston will always hold a special place in my heart for its beautiful beaches, incredibly friendly people, and rich history.

When Hubby got orders for San Diego, California, I also switched gears a bit and thought a grad school degree would be a good way to ensure a steady reporting job in a rocky newspaper market. Also, let's face it, the skill set of journalists and lawyers overlap quite a bit: you're usually trying to figure out what the truth is from a bunch of people, all of whom are probably lying to you.

Everyone thinks I spent most of my time in California lounging by the ocean, and in some ways I did. From the fourth floor of the law school library, if you looked out of the window from the right angle, you could just see San Diego Bay. That's about as close as I normally got.

By the time we got pregnant with Chloe, we were about to move again, this time to upstate New York. But I thought nothing could be as hard as law school, right?

Probably the first indication we had that this whole pregnancy thing was going to be intense happened as we were sitting in our living room in the San Diego suburbs, surrounded by a sea of hot wings and queso dip. Hubby and I are big football fans, and usually watching the

Superbowl is a party hard holiday. By the second half of the 2008 game, all the spandex started to blur into one for me. I mean, really, who wears that much spandex? It's neon colors, too. Only in the NFL can burly athletes get away with hot hooker pants.

Superbowl 2009 was a different story. As Hubby was enjoying a beer, munching some nachos and, I'm sure, musing upon some delightfully executed corner routes, he looked up suddenly when he noticed I was hysterically crying on the couch.

"What's wrong?" he said.

"It's ... It's just ..." I think I said, through a haze of tears.

"Are you ok? Are you sick?" he asked.

"The dogs ... they just helped out the Clydesdale, and ... it was so nice ... WAHHHHHH." I snorted, unable to finish, instead plunging my face into a tissue. Hubby was not sure how to handle this.

A few days later, Hubby's submarine deployed to the somewhere in the Pacific. At the time, we didn't know if he would be back in time for the baby's birth. For Lent, I decided to give up sex, alcohol and smoking. No, I've never actually smoked, but I felt like I should get credit for that, too.

My mood oscillated between outright elation to drama queen on prom night, as only massive doses of estrogen can elicit.

A few days after he deployed, I started studying full-time for California's February bar exam. I had tried getting out of taking the exam since I knew I was moving. It went something like this:

Me: So ... How about we skip this skip this whole bar thing?

School: One of the conditions of your scholarship is that you take the bar.

Me: Yeah, so ... it's a three-day, 18-hour test and California doesn't have reciprocity with any other state.

School: How would you like to owe $100,000?

Me: Hahahahahahahaha let's just forget I said anything. It'll be so much fun! The baby and I will have bar study parties!

Unfortunately, the bar also coincided with the Winter Olympics, which we all know is the greatest set of sporting events known to humankind. Yes, yes, that's not a typo. The Summer Olympics are *lame*. I'll prove it to you: No football — lame. No baseball anymore — lame. Instead of racing on ice or snow, where things are 10 times faster, people race on dry land — lame. And then there's speed walking. WALKING. As an Olympic sport. Don't get me started.

At the 2010 Winter Olympics, both U.S. ice hockey teams had a serious shot at gold, a historic moment in American sports.

When the U.S. women won the gold medal in 1998, it was a turning point. I had played hockey as a kid. My sister and I were always the only girls on the team. But then, in 1998, a girls' team started at my local rink — a 19-and-under team. We were so thinly spread that we literally had a 9-year-old and a 19-year-old.

Many years later I went back to the same rink when I was pregnant with Chloe and there were *seven* girls teams — U12, U16 and so forth — and there was a whole girls' high school league. So even the potential of seeing the women win it all again was electric. It was the hope of returning to that glory that had inspired so many young girls to succeed in the fastest sport on earth.

And the men were unstoppable, too. They beat Canada in the opening round, a feat no sports commentator had conceived. After finishing as the strongest team in the opening round, there were whispers of a repeat of the *Miracle on Ice* — that magic moment when the U.S. beat the Soviet Union in the 1980 Winter Olympics and we won it all. Sports Illustrated named it the best moment in U.S. sports history. It was a moment so mythical that the "Miracle" team got to light the torch at the Salt Lake City Olympics. It won us the Cold War. Or something like that.

As a lifelong hockey player and fan, born *after* this legend, it was the moment I had heard so much about but never got to experience. The Disney movie "Miracle" had come out just a few years before and I had gone to see it with my whole team. I was so looking forward to experiencing a triumph firsthand.

And so the moment came, the last week in February: Both the men's and the women's U.S. Olympic hockey teams had won their semifinals and were about to play their gold medal games. And I was going to take the California bar exam while five months pregnant — that magical time where you're both nauseated *and* have to pee constantly.

The first day, I did pretty well. I was actually pretty close to the bathroom, which helped when I had to run there every hour to pee. Well okay, I didn't run. It's more like I speed-walked. *Damn, I should be in the Summer Olympics!*

The second day, I threw up my breakfast and was feeling seriously queasy for the test. I looked at my antinausea medication bottle, which said "may cause drowsiness." Maybe not a medication you want to take right before the bar. I went back and forth for a while but eventually decided not to take it.

Thankfully, I actually did pretty well that day. Well, let me clarify — I gazed longingly at the nearest trash can every once in a while but restrained the urge to run over there.

I also wore my American University uniform, an outfit I considered appropriate for the occasion.

"Oh, wow, is that a hockey jersey?"

the proctor asked me as she handed out our tests.

"Yes, we're in the gold medal game," I said proudly. "And it doubles as great maternity wear, too."

She lowered her voice and started to whisper, as if I were in a prom dress and had just admitted to getting knocked up. "Are you pregnant?"

"Yes, of course," I said, visibly annoyed.

On the last day of the bar, the women played the gold medal game. And lost. Three days later, the men played the gold medal game. And lost. And I failed the bar. *Whomp whomp.*

Months later I realized what had happened. Since I knew I would be moving from California, it made much more sense for me to take tax law because, as it turns out, you have to pay your taxes every year, than Constitutional Law II, offered at the same time, though only tested on the California bar and really only practiced by a slim set of nonprofit attorneys.

I got a 1400 and needed a 1440 to pass — and I got exactly zero points on the Constitutional law essay. I thought, really, *zero* points? I went back to look at the essay and, wow, yes, I was way off — the obscure eminent domain topic they had referenced wasn't even *in* the 500-page-long study guide I had.

That's the logical reason, but then I think it makes much more sense framed behind the backdrop of unrequited hockey glory. Besides, eminent domain smacks of communist nationalization. Standing up against such oppression is why we fought the Soviets in hockey. Er, the Cold War. Something like that.

A few weeks after, I moved from California — first staying with family in Ohio and Pennsylvania in anticipation of our move to upstate New York in July.

At about nine months pregnant, I stopped by Wally World to pick up some new glasses, since I hadn't had my prescription updated in years.

I scoured row after row of a wall of sparkly new specs, but I could only find about five out of dozens that actually fit my face.

"Don't like our styles?" the clerk asked, surveying my pile of discards.

"Well, no, actually a lot of them are nice. It's just that very few fit my big head." I said. Then I looked down nervously at my chub, which doubled as a nice shelf. "You know, I'm starting to think this is a bad sign..."

A few days later, I was sitting at the pool suddenly I felt a big rush of liquid down under. Oh my God. This was go time.

We rushed to the hospital and got an overly enthusiastic nurse practitioner.

"Yes! Yes! This is probably it!" gushed Henny Penny, my newfound neonatal advocate. "Let's do the test to find out!"

She took a liquid sample and, sure enough, she pronounced me ready for an induction. This was the last thing I wanted to hear, since Hubby was finally off the submarine but still wrapping up things in California, and couldn't get back for another few days.

Thankfully, my mom had the sense to ask for someone else, and we got probably my favorite obstetrician there, a diminutive woman with a gentle smile and, in retrospect, rather large hands.

"Ah, yes," she said. "Well, we can

always double-check."

She snapped on a latex glove. Although she didn't, I noticed, go for the testing kit again. Instead, she was going to...

"AHHH!!"

It hurt like, well, sort of like what you think it would feel like if someone stuck their whole hand up your ass. She was up there for what seemed like an eternity before finally taking a step back.

"Don't worry," she said. "It's still intact."

I later learned the medical term for my condition: I believe it's called wetting your pants.

The baby was sitting unusually low on my pelvis, which means she was putting a lot of pressure on my bladder, which can lead to said unintentional incontinence. It's funny now, but somewhat awkward to describe when people ask why you went to the hospital.[1]

The night of July 4, I didn't get a lot of sleep. I kept waking up every half-hour

---

[1] Also, how did the nurse practitioner's test come up falsely positive? This was never explained to me.

or so having contractions. By breakfast, they were a little more regular but still pretty far apart. By lunch, they had quickened and at dinnertime even quicker still.

After dinner, every five minutes, my whole body would seize together. Suddenly I would feel an awful throbbing in my back like someone had jabbed in a bread knife and started to twist. This was really it. Go time. At about 10 p.m., we started for the hospital in a caravan — my husband, mother, father, brother, mother-in-law, father-in-law, brother-in-law and sister-in-law piled in two cars to start the one-hour trek there.

We arrived at the oversized lobby and waited while an attendant got us a wheelchair for the hike up to the third floor. Soon we were in the maternity ward again, facing a rather sour-faced middle-aged doctor who frowned while he read my charts.

"Yeah, you're only two centimeters dilated," he said, then stepped back to read the contraction meter strapped to my stomach.

I want to take a time out to go over what complete bullshit "centimeters dilated" means. For example, it implies there *centimeters* involved. It's like going into a chemistry lab, only to find out that they don't actually measure the chemicals, because that would be too much effort. Instead, they sort of eyeball it and hope nothing explodes. Oodles of birthing books go on about the stages of labor, detailing every stage by the number of centimeters dilated, without ever mentioning that the centimeters are, in fact, completely made up.

Granted, I may have only minored in science, but I'm pretty sure if I ever tried that in a science lab, the following would have transpired:

Me: So it looks here like you got, er, three centimeters.

University Professor: Um, no. Did you even use a ruler?

Me: Ruler Schmuler. I'm sure it's three centimeters, that's my best guess.

Professor: Um, yeah centimeters are actually based on the SI system of measurement.

Me: Don't you try being one of these hippie metric freaks now.

Professor: .... And you fail.

So I got to the hospital, expecting

them to reach for some sort of small measuring device ... and instead got a hand up my ass.

"Yes, but how do you know I'm only two centimeters dilated?" I asked. "You didn't measure."

"We don't actually measure, we estimate by the tip of our fingers," he said, as if stating the most obvious thing in the world.

I have of course, since come up with many witty comebacks in my head, like perhaps, "Okay then, if we're being so precise, we'll pay our hospital bill on the eleventeenth of two thousand never."

But at the time, I was so shocked that no one bothered to stock sophisticated scientific equipment like, say, a ruler, that I didn't know what to say.

"You aren't far enough along, so we're going to have to send you home."

"But I'm in a lot of pain! Can I have an epidural?" I said.

The doctor sighed and took a look at the nurse, who at this point was equally annoyed with She-Who-Wets-Her-Pants-and-Thinks-Silly-Things-Like-Measurements-Should-be-Taken-in-Hospitals.

"You're not in a lot of pain," she said. "A lot of first time mothers think they're in a lot of pain."

"No, no, no, I'm in a lot, I mean a LOT of pain," I said, now pleading desperately to make the back stabbing stop.

"The baby will probably come in the next few days," the doctor said, as if ignoring the requests of a painkiller addict. "Right now, you're not in labor."

"DAYS?" I repeated, incredulous. This was going to be horrible.

So at about 10:30 p.m. we went home, and everyone else went to sleep. Except for me, of course, because I was being repeatedly STABBED in the back, and Hubby who started to watch reruns on TV.

The pain went from something absolutely unbearable, just totally, terribly, horribly, wrenchingly awful to something I can't even describe because it was much, much worse. I couldn't sit or stand anymore. I was in a ball on the floor screaming bloody murder during each contraction, and moaning during the ever-briefer seconds in between.

The pain was so bad that I started

to "white out"— the edges of my field of vision would become translucent and get closer to the center so that during the most painful moments I couldn't see a thing. This went on for what seemed like an eternity, an alternation of pain, moans, "whiting out" and nonstop "That '70s Show" in the background.

At about 3 a.m., I started to throw up and couldn't stop throwing up. This started to get Hubby concerned. I, on the other hand, was totally nonplussed — yakking while in labor is like getting a bee sting after a compound fracture. It would hurt a lot normally, but after a bone is sticking through your flesh, a bee sting barely moves the needle. I did, however, agree with him that I needed to go back to the hospital. I figured if I wasn't having a baby, I was, at the very least, dying.

So, once again, Team Labor assembled, this time with a groggy catcher and a few straggly basemen, while the others promised to catch up in the next inning.

Sometime towards the end of the trip, I got a sudden feeling. I can't explain it quite, but all of the sudden I had to push. I just HAD to. For reasons I am eternally grateful, my car has a side handle, and I held on to it for dear life as I started pushing with all of my might. Thankfully there weren't any cars on the road at 3:30 a.m. or I can only imagine passing drivers would be confused by the woman pulled up tight on the handlebar, Tarzan-style, bellowing an appropriate jungle call: "Aaaaah AHHHHH!"

We pulled up to the now-empty lobby as fast as we could. The wait for a wheelchair was the shortest yet the longest time I could possibly imagine.

We finally made it to the maternity ward, where infamous Doc McGruffins greeted us.

"Hmm, you're nine centimeters[2] dilated," he said, after performing my exam. "I don't think we can do an epidural."

I don't remember the particulars of the conversation that followed, since I was in and out of consciousness and my grip on reality at this point was tenuous at best. But I do remember the doctor's

---

[2] Also, how can you be nine centimeters dilated and pushing? Pushing only happens after you're fully dilated, i.e. "10 centimeters" and... Argh I give up.

rather novel theory that I had just happened to go into labor the second I got home, and the wrath of my mother erupting like a miniature Mount St. Helens. In the end, he decided that I might be able to get an epidural.

The anesthesiologist had to time the needle carefully to go in between my pushes, which at this point were wracking my body uncontrollably. But finally the pain started to fade and I had the best three-hour nap of my life.

When I woke up early the next morning, there had been a shift change, and thankfully a much more agreeable obstetrician had arrived, although behind her lurked the ninja.

The ninja was an older, scruffy-haired, permanently frown-faced nurse who made it clear that the morning wasn't really her favorite time of day.

"Yes, I think we slowed it down too much, you're not pushing well enough. We're going to turn off the epidural," She said.

Off, as in OFF. Not down. She made it clear my input was not wanted or needed.

"No, no, NO!" I cried. "I can push

harder, I swear." But this didn't seem to appease her.

Suddenly the magic drip was gone, and the fire between my legs came back again. I was pushing, and pushing, and pushing, each squeeze a more horrific undertaking than the last. The baby's head was starting to come through, but she didn't seem to want to go all the way.

"Hmm," said the Ninja Nurse, putting on a glove. "Let me see if I can help."

Without warning or explanation, she reached down and pushed back the skin around the baby's head. I could literally feel myself being torn apart. It was like feeling a part of your body on fire and then having someone add extra coal to the flames.

"YeeeAHHHH NO DON'T DO THAT!" I shrieked.

She was nonplussed. "We have to help the baby come through," she snorted and then trotted off, I'm assuming to find another victim.

I pushed and pushed and pushed. Finally, I had reached my limit and I was spent. I just couldn't do it anymore. The sweat was dripping down my back and I felt exhausted in every part of my being. It was nearly 1 p.m. in the afternoon and I had been running this marathon for hours. I just I wanted to scream, "I have to take a break! I can't do this anymore!"

And at the very moment that I had given up, when I just couldn't do it anymore because I had no energy left, that's when Cleopatra Joan entered the world.

All eyes in the room turned to that one tiny face as she opened her eyes for the first time and let out a primordial scream. I tried to grab a look, too, but that's when I felt the first karate chop.

Literally 10 seconds after the birth, the nimble Ninja Nurse laid into me with some moves that would have made Jackie Chan jealous.

"WHAT ARE YOU DOING?" I cried, equally angry and scared.

Ninja Nurse offered no explanation, warning or sympathy. Instead, she sized up the situation and, with a tone that I'm guessing she reserved for the particularly simple-minded, she told me, "We have to get the blood out."

Chloe was born with meconium all over her. Which, as it turns out, is a fancy medical term for poop. This really should have been our first indication that she was a super-duper pooper, but I digress. When my water finally broke at the hospital, it was laden with tiny baby crap, and so when she was first born, a neonatal team whisked her away to make sure she didn't inhale any bacteria floating around in there.

So as my mother, husband, mother-in-law and most others flocked to the baby (as they should), I was left to the obstetrician, who was bent over, busily trying to stitch me up, and the Ninja Nurse, who at this point was getting a Kill Bill thrill out of it.

"Stop!" I cried, but meeker, given the futility of the situation.

Finally, after a long time they brought the baby back to me. "Chloe" was a sight to behold. She had fairly long jet-black hair, long fingers and a scraggly skin. And a head, of course, literally in the 95th to 100th percentile.

She took one look at me and I could tell she loved me.

Well, sort of. She kept looking around until she found what she was really looking for — boobies.

Chapter 2: Rochester and the Boobie Conspiracy

We moved to Rochester, New York, about three weeks after Chloe was born. Because right after the most physically draining event of my life seemed a good time to rearrange everything I've ever owned.

If New York were a hockey skate,[3] Rochester would be on the laces. On average, it is the third snowiest city in the U.S., according to the Weather Channel's statistics, coming in at about 100.5 inches per year. It's close behind number one Syracuse, which is just an hour east of Rochester. With an average of just 0.3 inches more per year, Erie, Pennsylvania, ranks number two. Number four is Buffalo, New York, an hour west of Rochester. And yes, these climate cousins, dotted along the Great Lakes, all rank higher than number five — Anchorage, Alaska. ALASKA.

In Rochester, the snow comes early and often, but there is a surreal beauty to

---

[3] Granted the blade of the skate, Long Island, is a bit off but then a shoe would just be too boring.

it. Lake effect snow is not like snow farther south. It's much lighter, and it has an almost airy quality. You go out in the morning after a fresh coat and everything is a pristine white, as if brushed with a fine pixie dust to smooth out the landscape. It inspires wonder in a way that few natural phenomena can.

The University of Rochester is happy to boast that storms have closed the school just six times since the end of World War II, despite its faux polar locale. If Rochester had a hashtag, it would be #DealWithIt. If it rains, bring an umbrella. If it snows, shovel the walk. If someone ran into a house and shouted "Fire!" my guess is 9 out of 10 Americans would panic. Those from Rochester would calmly exit the building.

I remember the first hockey game I went to in the snow. It was nearly a blizzard outside. I wanted to call the captain of the team, but then I didn't want to be the dumb Southerner who couldn't handle a little winter. I nearly turned back several times, fearing my own timidity had turned to stupidity. But, sure enough, when I arrived there with all my gear, the parking lot was full. No one in the locker room asked if the game would be canceled or even mentioned the weather at all.

Snow makes life quite a bit more complicated, though, if you have a baby and share a one-car garage. On days that my car was outside, I would have to wait for Chloe's first nap time, then go outside and dig out the car. Because as it turns out, babies do not enjoy waiting in their car seat in freezing weather while you get things situated.

I would then wait for her second nap to warm up the car, and then put her in there to go to the store, all the while praying that an icy wind would not wake her up on the way to the backseat. You do not, *do not* want to attempt a misguided sojourn into the great outdoors with a screaming baby. Then you're caged with the tiger. The only thing that seemed to calm her was milk, and I couldn't breastfeed her in a car seat.

I'm really not a fan of what I like to call the boobie conspiracy.

I'd like to back up a minute and note that I get exactly zero dollars from formula companies and that there's a plethora of research out there backing up the notion that breastmilk is much better for babies. I don't dispute that, and really it makes sense. If you had a bowl of mac and cheese from a box every day, that couldn't be good for you either. (Also, I mean really, there are not a whole lot of things in nature that are neon orange.) So there is my lecture … do as I say, not as I do.

After a while, I realized that, for me, breastfeeding was a terrible idea. I have a nice breast pump, but one thing I hadn't counted on is that if you breastfeed, say, every six hours or whatever, you're going to get really full every six hours. So if you're silly enough to think you're going to skip a feeding and let someone else feed the baby from a pre-pumped bottle, you will instead wake from your much-needed slumber with a chestful of agony. A bursting boob is like someone taking the most sensitive part of your body and ratcheting up the pressure. (Although, neat parlor trick: If you happen to have your shirt off and the baby cries, your brain will subconsciously open the floodgates, as it were, and suddenly you are a high-powered Austin Powers fem-bot, although sadly you only shoot milk.)

And let's just skip all this nonsense about bonding with your baby while breastfeeding. If anything, you feel less bonded to her. You just want to hold your baby in your arms and look on that really tiny, really cute face. But you can't. Every time you hold her, she does her best little sea lion *flop flop* until she can score some milk.

Another thing I hadn't counted on was the fact that I would leak all the time. At first I used some cheap cotton breastfeeding pads, but they would just swell enormously and add to the mounting pressure problem anytime I was about to feed. In the end, I found pads that wicked the moisture away, which was super helpful, but of course they were very expensive: essentially, boob diapers.

But in those early days, when I was much more concerned with "Mother of the Year" than my sanity, I decided to breastfeed Chloe, at least for a while.

I've done a lot of crazy things while tired. I've poured my orange juice into my cereal bowl. I've spilled coffee on my shirt because I brought the cup to my mouth with the opening on the side and not the bottom. At the nadir of my semiconsciousness, I actually poured boiling water not into my teacup, but onto my hand beside it. That moment seemed to go in slow motion as I began to pour the tea and some part of my brain started to realize *"hmm, I don't think I'm actually pouring this into the cup ... owwwww."* Though, conveniently, that really woke me up.

All these feats of clouded cognition I've just described came *before* I had a baby, just your average night of staying up a little too late.

So after Chloe was born, feeding her around the clock kept me in a fuzzy state of consciousness. I watched a lot of Star Trek reruns in the wee morning hours. Captain Jean Luc Picard has a badass quality to him that I never really appreciated the first time I watched the show. I also watched a lot of infomercials. I nearly bought a Slap Chop at 3 a.m. Because anything you hear about after 1 a.m. sounds awesome.

Chloe grew from the 10th percentile to the 25th percentile to the 50th percentile for weight. Her hair faded to a chestnut brown and her legs started to adorably chunk. She would feed for 45 minutes on a side, every three to four hours, from the *start* of the previous feeding.

I knew that was too long, and that I was, in an unhealthy way, her comfort blanket of sorts, but she wouldn't take a pacifier and I didn't really know any other way to make her happy. I mean, God knows I tried. She would cry, so I would pick her up, and then *flop flop flop* she would find her way to some milk. Man those sea lions are fast.

"I think we need a Shark Vac," I told my husband one day over dinner. "I saw it on an infomercial at 4 a.m. It cleans really well."

"Um, yeah I don't know about that," he said. "You've never been a big cleaner."

"Yes, but there's no harsh abrasives!" I said.

"Um, okay. Did you go to the store to pick up bread?"

"Yes, I did! I dug the car out, then I put her in there, she didn't wake up, it was great!"

"Did you pick up milk, too?"

"Oh. No. I forgot that," I said, dejected. "Well, I guess that's a project for all of tomorrow ..."

"What are these?" He asked, rifling through the store bags.

"Oh, those are really awesome. They're diapers."

"They don't look like diapers."

"Oh, right. They're diapers for me."

"For you?"

"Yes. For my boobs. They work great."

"Hmm. Okay."

"SO much better than the cotton pads."

"Uh, right. Just what I was thinking," he said. "By the way, have you seen my blue Navy Sailing shirt? Lucia? Lucia?"

"Huh, what?" I said, waking up, startled. "It's actually the Romulans! They just want you to *think* it's the Klingons."

"Um, maybe you shouldn't be feeding her right now," he said.

"Oh, no, it's okay." I said. "I can totally eat with one hand. I define my diet right now as that which I can eat one-handed."

"No, I mean you shouldn't feed her and then fall asleep. You could drop her," he said.

"Oh, no, I wasn't falling asleep, I

was just resting my eyes for a minute. I actually just saw that Star Trek. Or maybe I dreamed it ... Actually, I'm not sure right now."

"Um ... Right." he said. "So, about my Navy Sailing shirt. Have you seen it?"

"Ah, yes. I have. It was upstairs in the box on the corner. No, maybe I hung it up after taking it out of the boxes in the downstairs closet. Or it could be in the other room. Actually, I'm not sure."

I celebrated the end of the boobie conspiracy six months after I started with my very first 8-hour stretch of sleep. It took me a long time to actually wean her, though. She did not want to take a bottle for the longest time, and there were many panicked phone calls to my mother where I wailed that she would be breastfeeding in college. Finally, Hubby got her to take a bottle, though, which saved me a lot of frustration and a rather awkward trip to a university admissions office.

During the weaning period, it was about 4 a.m. at some point in early January when Chloe woke up and I was trying to get her to go back to sleep instead of feeding her. For the first time in her life, she indicated a purposeful word.

"MILK!" She signed, clear as day, just as I had been trying to teach her for a long time in sign language. *Aw man, now I have to reinforce the concept.* I thought. *Well, maybe she didn't really mean to do it.*

"MILK!" She signed again, this time shoving her hand as close as possible to my face. "MILK!"

Chapter 3: Sign Language

I am a big proponent of sign language. I have used it with both my girls, and it really helped them to understand things faster. Although, once they talk, they talk back, and things just go downhill from there, really.

I'm also a fan of teaching colors early. You know, so they can sort laundry. But I digress.

When I first saw a friend's child — a BABY— ask her parents for things in sign language, it blew my mind. I had never seen anyone that small who was able to communicate. So when Chloe got old enough, we took out all the baby sign language DVDs from the library and eventually bought them because we had so much success.

Sign language is also really important because when they do talk, half the time it's impossible to tell what they're saying. The first day Chloe said "love you" was also the first day she dropped the F-bomb. However, after a few minutes of horror/giggling, I realized she was actually (probably? hopefully?) doing her chicken impression with her chicken dance toy and the "CL" in "cluck" eluded her.

There's really a pre-talking phase when they mimic the sounds in their barnyard books — "baa," "moo" and the like. Then it moves on to a slurred speech that starts to sound like language. When Chloe was 2, I wrote down some of her toddler-ese translations: *Teddy Bear = Diddy Baye. Strawberries = Bobbies. Boobies = blueberries or actual boobies, depending on the context. Mo = More. Vegetables = NO! Cheese = Dee. Hockey = och ee. Up = uppy. (Neighbor kid) Peter = pee pee.*

Sometimes, even when you know what your kid is saying, it's not very helpful if they don't speak in sentences. For example, when your kid says, "NOSE,

NOSE!" you may not want to inspect the nose up close to see what's wrong because it could also mean she's about to sneeze.

"Sorry, mom," Chloe said, pointing at some boogers she just ejected. "I got some Bless You right here."

Chetta's first sign was also "milk," although at first she thought it meant all food. So when I fed her yogurt or whatever and I took a break, she would shove a squeezing hand in my face, as if to say, "SHOVEL FASTER, MINION."

Although, even with sign language, sometimes it's hard to figure out what they're saying, particularly if a sign's complexity supersedes their manual dexterity. For example, one day I signed and said "bath" and Cleopatra got excited and walked all the way to the bathtub and climbed in it. Turns out she had been signing "bath" for a while, but I didn't realize because instead of scrubbing her chest, her version was more like "grab your bitty baby boobies."

Diary of a Teddy, Part 1:
6 a.m.: Jolted awake as I'm thrown headfirst from crib.

6:30 a.m.: Head poked repeatedly with a comb as Chloe attempts to brush me.

7 a.m.: Face smushed into window as Chloe shows me the pretty white "no" outside that fell last night.

8 a.m.: Moisturized. That feels good, actually.

10 a.m.: Invited to tea party with Chloe and that loser Elmo.

11 a.m.: Nap.

1 p.m.: I get to eat "bobbies" for lunch.

2 p.m.: Everyone is wearing socks, so Chloe puts socks on me.

4 p.m.: Gah, who keeps pushing Elmo's button?

7 p.m.: Storytime. Ooh, I like this one, it has bears in it. That blondie porridge thief had it coming!

7:30 p.m.: Cuddle with Chloe time. This is so worth it.

Chapter 4: Bar Exam Numero Dos

One day, while I was sitting quietly in a public place reading a book, I overheard a loud phone call from the lady behind me. I learned during this call that she disapproved of those young kids who are always on their phones. I learned this during the hour-long call she took in the LIBRARY.

Since I had Chloe in the summer of 2010, I waited until the next year to take the New York bar. So most of the summer of 2011 my mom took Chloe to the pool and I stayed in the library working on problems such as this (from my bar review essay book):

"On a beautiful day in the fall of 2001, Chuck, who was married to another, moved into Martha's home ... and became her lover. At various times when they were

living together, Martha advanced money to Chuck as follows:" [Blah Blah Blah she lends him money, then surprise, surprise he doesn't pay her back and moves in with another woman.]

Of course, I was left wondering the obvious question: why was it a beautiful fall day?

This time, thankfully, I passed the bar, and in the winter started working part-time for an awesome sole practitioner lawyer in Rochester, while also doing some freelance reporting.

Part II: Virginny

Chapter 5: I like to move it, move it

Hubby had enjoyed his time in the Navy but with a toddler, I needed his help a lot more. Also, he had just earned his MBA and wanted to try the wild world of finance.

He got a job offer in McLean, Virginia, a suburb of Washington, D.C., and we moved to nearby Vienna in the summer of 2012. I was very familiar with the area, having gone to college nearby, though needless to say my priorities had changed a little. Suddenly "where are all the good bars?" was not as important as "where are all the good parks?"

We moved into a house that a 90-year-old woman had just moved out of because we thought the optimal design aesthetic should be "What would Michael Jackson do?"

Our new house featured toilets of every color: green, yellow, and of course, pink. A bold fuchsia wrapped around the living room, and I'm pretty sure our stair carpet came from the hide of a Wookie. The house had an excellent location, though, and even a bit of backyard, which is hard to find so close to the city.

Northern Virginia is a booming area, thanks to the rapid and relatively recent rise of Washington, D.C. According to Census Bureau Data, the D.C. area has grown 25 percent in the past 15 years, and it is now the sixth largest metropolitan area in the US.

A friend of mine once said that every eighth grade class president grows up and moves to D.C., which is probably close to the truth. It is a wonderful and unique city because every street is filled with the National Center for This or That, and the downtown area is clean and centered around a beautiful historical park.

There are of course the famous sites, such as the Smithsonian, the U.S. Botanical Garden, the Newseum and the Library of Congress. There's also a wonderful variety of smaller museums and organizations, each promoting their own slice of scientific or intellectual achievement: there's the National Museum of Health and Medicine, featuring the bullet that killed Lincoln; the International Spy Museum which boasts the famous Enigma cipher machine; and the National Society of the United States Daughters of 1812, which wins props for having the mast of the U.S.S. Constitution, "Old Ironsides," and of course for challenging Americans to remember that we actually fought a war in 1812.

Particularly interesting is the Hillwood Estate, Museum and Gardens, tucked into an obscure corner of Northwest Washington. It was the main mansion of Marjorie Merriweather Post, who, at 27, became heiress to the Post Cereal Company (later General Foods of your breakfast fame). At one time the wealthiest woman in the world, Post developed expensive taste in art, starting with French antiques, and the Hillwood collection features over 17,000 of her prizes.

Of particular fame, though, is the Russian collection. Post accompanied her third husband, Joseph Davies, to the Soviet Union in the 1930s where he worked as ambassador. There she snapped up treasures that once belonged to the recently unseated Russian aristocracy, in some cases buying directly from the Soviet government, which had nationalized many items. Stalin financed some of his anti-capitalist dreams by selling to one of the world's great capitalists, ironically.

I tried to take the kids to see the museums as often as I could. When we first arrived, I took Chloe downtown to see the Smitsonian's Air and Space Museum.

"It's going to be really cool. We're going to see real rockets!" I promised.

We took the Metro downtown, which was probably the highlight for Chloe.

"Oh, wow, a train!" she cried. And then, "We're going through a tunnel!" once we reached the city limits.

After reaching our stop, we walked a few blocks, went all the way around to the handicap entrance so we could get in with the stroller, and waited patiently in the security line, ostensibly with America's future astronauts.

Finally, we reached the atrium, an enormous hall probably four stories high filled with great planes, rockets and aeronautical oddities. Chloe looked up with wonder, taking in the massive scale of the objects around her. I sauntered over to the center of the room, proud of myself for introducing my young progeny to the wonders of science.

"And this," I said prosaically, touching a saucer-like spaceship, "went to the moon. Astronauts landed on the moon and then came back in this. Maybe we can go see the moon rocks next."

"Yeah!" Chloe said. "When do we go to the moon?"

"What? Oh honey, we're not going to the moon."

"We're *not* going to the moon?" she said, incredulous. "You said the rockets were real!"

"Well, yes... they are real. But you have to be an astronaut," I said realizing I did not explain this right. "Maybe you can be an astronaut someday."

"NOOOOO, I want to go to space! You said we could go to space!" she wailed. Buckets of tears followed.

And that is what we like to call crashing and burning.

Chapter 6: Having a Second Kid

Getting pregnant with your first child is like, "Oh, my gosh! We've created life! We're going to be parents!" Having a second child is more like, "When does this thing hatch so I can get back to my vices?"

A few weeks after Chloe was born, *Time* magazine ran an article featuring the benefits of only children. I read it and totally understood. Though we had originally agreed to have more, Hubby and I decided, with newborn Chloe, that she would definitely be an only child. I mean, anyone who could do this kid thing multiple times was just nuts, right?

About a year and a half later, while having dinner, we began to revisit the issue.

"Want to come play now?" said Chloe.

"No, honey, Mommy is still eating dinner."

"Okay, how about now?"

"No, I'm still eating."

"Okay, Daddy, want to come play?"

"I'm still eating, Chloe," Hubby said.

"Oh, okay. Mommy are you done yet?"

After about the 423rd iteration of this, it began to dawn on us that maybe she needed a playmate, or perhaps maybe we needed her to need a playmate, or else there was a good chance we would starve.

Also, Chloe has Hubby's blood type. And what if I need a kidney someday?

Having Concetta was different in many ways. Though moving, like having a baby, always seems like a good idea until the heavy labor.

Right after we moved to Virginia, since I was six months pregnant, I decided it would be a good idea to do the hospital tour. But as it turns out, the hospital didn't give out maps. Because really, why focus on a silly thing like letting people know where they are going?

On the tour I did get a large full-color pamphlet, though, filled with smiling happy photographs of models who very clearly did not just give birth, holding infants who very clearly were not newborns, and I even got a 10 percent off coupon for baby merchandise. You know, just in case I found time to go shopping while in labor. Too bad that, without a map, I was never able to find my way to the gift shop.

Chloe and Chetta also moved in different ways, which surprised me quite a bit. Chloe loved to flip around in utero, while she was still small enough to do so. I would wake up suddenly in the middle of the night because I kept having dreams that she was falling off of something. But actually, it was just her twirling around in there like so many spacewalking astronauts.

Chetta and Tiny T3 prefer to expand out and not around. With Chetta constantly dancing a jig in there, I was fairly certain I was about to give birth to an international pop star. Though I wasn't quite as excited each time there was another moonwalk across my bladder.

And the last part of the pregnancy was painful. Mostly because I burned my finger on a Pop Tart. But really, when else in your life can you eat pastry without guilt?

By the end of my pregnancy with Chetta, I had to pee about every hour, but for some reason I never considered how difficult it would be with a toddler when I was constantly in the bathroom. By the time Chetta was regularly using my bladder as a trampoline, pretty much any time I went anywhere with Chloe the following scene unfolded:

Me, trying to squeeze my big ol'

belly into a bathroom stall: "Okay, come in here with mommy. And don't touch anything."

"What this?" said Chloe, lifting up the lid to the tiny trash can.

"UGH THAT'S GROSS! Um, just please don't touch it."

"What's that?" said Chloe, trying to reach for a used pad.

"NO! DIRTY!" I screamed, grabbing her hand. And then she would cry uncontrollably, just in time for me to try to waddle out past a sobbing toddler who now did not want to move or go anywhere.

Chapter 7: A Bar, a Wedding and a Funeral

Late in the winter of 1919, in a crowded row home in South Philadelphia, a baby was born to a family of Italian immigrants. She was born on a special day: December 13, the feast of Saint Lucia, (Loo-chee-ah) the patron saint of Light. So they named her after the saint. If not, she apparently would have been Yolanda. I think we both dodged a bullet on that one.

When she went to school, her teachers decided that Lucia was "too ethnic" and so she went by "Lucy" for most of her life. She wasn't able to stay in school for long, though, in a family of 13 children. She was working in a factory when she met my grandfather, an Italian immigrant who also had to leave school early to work on the docks. They ran away to elope because they couldn't afford a big wedding.

My grandfather also specialized in light. He started a business manufacturing and selling lamps and eventually built his own factory. Together they had a family and eventually moved out to the suburbs. In her 40s, my grandmother finally got her driver's license.

But though you can take the girl out of South Philly, you can't take the South Philly out of the girl. She always retained her thick accent and practical sensibilities. She didn't drink much and rarely smoked, unlike her peers. But she always loved playing the lottery and going to the "casina."

When I think back on my grandmother, it's not the big things that strike me, but rather the little things. I remember that she tripped once and I thought she would get upset but she didn't. Instead, she started laughing uncontrollably. It's reminded me to laugh at all my stumbles, both literal and otherwise. If I could be just half of the mother that my grandmother Lucy was, then I would consider myself a success. Also, she had six kids, a feat which seems incredible to me right now with only three.

And she only misplaced one kid just one time, which really, given the mayhem of six offspring, is not bad at all. Despite being lost, my mother figured out how to walk that mile home anyway, so really no big deal. After finally reaching their house, instead of announcing her return, my mother, just 5 years old and already a smartass herself, went up to my grandmother and offered a sarcastic, "Thanks a lot, mom."

My grandmother looked up. "For what?"

"For leaving me at the store!"
"Oh!"

By the age of 92, I could tell her mind was starting to go. But for someone her age, she really was quite with it.

"Hello?" she answered the phone one day while I was pregnant with Chetta.

"Gramom it's me!"

"Who is this?"

"It's your favorite granddaughter."

"Carla?"

"Um, no. Though I suppose I deserved that. It's me, Lucia."

"Oh, Lucia, Lucia! Yes. How yous doin'?"

"Good. The baby is getting really big."

"Is the baby walking yet?"

"Um, no." I hesitated. "Also, I'm still pregnant."

"Okay."

"But I have a good number for you."

"You do!"

"Yes, our new address."

"Okay, thanks honey, I'll go play it."

The last time I was able to speak on the phone with her, I was again studying for the bar, this time the Virginia bar since we had just moved to the D.C. area. Though New York and Virginia have reciprocity, I hadn't worked there long enough to waive in, and so yet again I found myself a prisoner of the library.

My plans to study, though, were cut short when, in early July, my grandmother had a massive stroke. I remember standing there, holding her hand, which had been paralyzed by the stroke, while watching the life slowly fading out of her other half as well. Then I put a penny in her clenched hand for good luck. She would have wanted it that way.

The rest of July was a blur to me, filled with my relatives going back and forth to my grandmother in hospice, my trying to cram for the bar exam, and preparations to fly to Ohio where my sister-in-law was getting married (and Hubby and Chloe were in the wedding).

And so, while teetering on the edge of my third trimester, we drove to Philly for the funeral to say goodbye to my grandmother.

"I know what love is," Chloe told me confidently one day.

"Oh?" I said.

"It's like kissing and hugging and stuff," she said with a matter-of-fact tone. "But..." she trailed off, as if lost in thought. "It's crying, too. Like when you love someone so much and you cry when they leave."

"Yes," I said. "It's like that, too."

I drove to Roanoke, Virginia, to take the bar, because why have a bar exam in the most populated part of the state when you can inconvenience everyone with a fun road trip to nowhere?

At the end of the week, we got to the wedding. *Finally, I can relax,* I thought. But Chloe had other plans.

Oh the day of the wedding, Chloe was all set in her flower girl dress and I had wrangled her into place at the church. Through a mix-up at the hotel, I had accidentally put on my flip flops and I was starting to feel sick because, you know, I was very very pregnant and had stupidly only had a granola bar for lunch. When the doors finally opened, Chloe took one look around and froze. Yes, Cleopatra Joan, who has never had a shy moment of her life, who goes up to kids on the playground and says "hi, friends!", who talks to strangers in the bathroom stall next to her – yes, that kid got cold feet when it was her turn to walk up the aisle.

And so with Chloe not budging and my father-in-law urging me to just pick her up, I inadvertently secured an unwanted place in the spotlight myself.

I now maintain that this was all a ploy to make the bride look better, though she certainly did not need any help from me to look good. But it helps a bit if you are preceded by a fat cow with hippie shoes who is holding a cowering toddler and trying to catch up to the ring bearer and other flower girl.

Chloe did much, much better though at the reception.

"I'M DANCING!" she kept screaming as she ran in circles on the dance floor.

All night she ran around, having the time of her life. She had a white a dress on with a blue bow, in a room filled with chairs decorated with white covers and similar blue bows. She kept blending in and we lost her a few times. But it all turned out OK because thankfully she was going at such as high speed that no one could sit on her.

Chapter 8: Baby Sister

With Concetta, the doctor actually

induced me because, according to my medical chart, I had a history of "fast labor." I tried explaining that I highly doubted I had "fast labor" because the first doctor's theory that I had magically gone into labor the second he sent me home from the hospital seemed rather suspect. And I'm sure he was much more likely to write "fast labor" in my medical file than "doctor was a complete moron."

Still, in the interest of avoiding even the possibility of another 3 a.m. fright fest with me screaming and pushing in the car, I agreed. And so on a quiet morning in late October 2012, we found ourselves all set up in the hospital room, without any drama.

Well, of course, there's always *some* drama when having a baby. For six hours, it went pretty well, but then for the next six hours I didn't dilate any more. Because of umbilical cord issues, I ended up having an emergency C-section.

It wasn't ideal, but it worked out, and the overall the experience was the complete opposite of what I had with Chloe. The doctor was friendly and supportive. No nurses had unfulfilled ju-jitsu aspirations. Everyone let me know what they were going to do before they did it. And strangely enough, everyone assumed a grown woman was competent enough to assess her own pain level, not that I had much pain at all.

We wheeled into the operating room and several minutes later, I heard a reassuring wail as the doctor brought Concetta into the world. A nurse brought her over so that Hubby and I could see her. She was not at all what I expected: this one was all her daddy. She had blue eyes, fair skin, and a shock of bleach blond hair. I was so happy I cried.

As soon as we brought her home, Chloe loved the new baby dearly. We really had to keep an eye on Chloe because she kept bringing over toys for her new playmate, who was usually sleeping in her bouncer. I was afraid Chetta wouldn't be able to breathe as she was slowly buried in a mountain of stuffed animals.

"HI BABY SISTER! I GOT YOU A RATTLE! OPEN YOUR HAND, BABY SISTER! OPEN YOUR HAND!" the overly friendly giant would shout.

Other times, she would draw

pictures for her new little friend.

"CHETTA! LOOK WHAT I DREW! CHETTA! CLAP FOR ME!"

Chloe started a new favorite game of "pretend"— she would dress up her teddy bear and baby doll in diapers and walk them around in her stroller. Teddy is a "baby brudder," Chloe explained to me, because he doesn't talk. Just like her baby sister didn't talk. In fact the only thing she wanted for Christmas was a bottle for her baby dolls. Slowly she became a new "expert" on raising a baby.

"Babies cry sometimes," she explained to me. "Yes. But it's okay. I get her tissue."

When my mother-in-law, holding and looking at the baby, asked, "How about we walk around a bit?" Chloe's face went white with panic.

"No!" she cried. "She can't walk!"

Newborn Chetta never really liked the bouncer chair much, or the play gym. She only liked the Baby Bjorn. But then, wouldn't you want to take a nap while motorboating everything that you love?

According to my handy dandy nursing timer app, and not counting when I pumped every day so Hubby could help, too, Concetta had 60 feedings in her first full week, for a total of 39.7 hours. Cow duty is a full-time job. Keep in mind that doesn't include burping, diaper changing or bathing the kid.

I have the upmost respect for breastfeeding mothers who have more than one child. I have no idea how they can be up all night with one, then up all day with another and still function. By the end of a month, I had had enough. And so with absolute elation and quivering dread I stopped breastfeeding Chetta.

Diary of the Baby, Part 1:
Morning: Slept. Woke up. Famished. Had some milk. Milk taken away. MAD FACES. Burped. That feels better actually. Dressed in purple. WHY WOULD I WEAR PURPLE WHEN I FEEL LIKE WEARING PINK? Yakked on purple. Now dressed in pink.

Afternoon: Slept. Buried in stuff animals by overly friendly giant. Pooped. Reloaded. Pooped. Reloaded. Pooped.

Night: Bathtime. Contemplated meaning of life and pretty shiny thing above. Dressed in blue pajamas. BUT I

WANT PINK. Had delightful explosive poop. Now dressed in pink pajamas. Ahh. Have decided that parents are delightful and easily trained. Used one as pillow for evening nap. Slept.

Chapter 9: Say the Magic Words

I passed the Virginia bar exam, too, and in October of 2012 received my invitation to get sworn in. Swearing in is a rather formal affair steeped in tradition, which is code for "it makes no sense, but we've been doing it for hundreds of years so we'll keep doing it anyway." Basically, in order to actually practice before a state court, you have to go say the magic words before the Supreme Court of Virginia.

You'd think this communal knighthood would take place in the part of Virginia with the largest population — the Washington, D.C. area. But you would be wrong. All official business takes place in the state capital, an absurdity that I've never quite come to grips with — New York lawyers aren't required to go to Albany for anything. I'm fairly certain half of them don't know Albany *is* the capital.

I called the Virginia State Bar and tried explaining that, well you know, I had just finished giving birth and I had already sworn to uphold the Constitution in New York, so maybe I could pass on this Richmond road trip idea? They said they totally understood and that I could come down later as long as I had a sponsor in Richmond (a city where I knew zero people) or I could swear in at a local court. Although in a local court, my pledge to uphold the Constitution and something about Justice and Liberty and all these good things would only be limited to *that* court. Whereas, if you say your oath before the highest court, it transfers to all other courts. Naturally.

And so I made the trek down to Richmond with a still-breastfeeding 1-month-old. I entered a grand ballroom at the Richmond Convention Center, which had been decked out for the occasion as an official session of the Virginia Supreme Court. A row of elevated seats lined the stage, and a group of solemn old lawyers sat in their seats, donning their official black robes. The Virginia State Seal displayed prominently above, the soldier of righteousness over a freshly murdered tyrant.

The audience was a mass of fresh-faced new attorneys, all lined up in neat rows sporting their new black suits. In the very back row, one tiny baby sat dressed in bright white with green flowers.

The crowd grew silent for the speaker, who had started on a long lecture extolling the virtues of the law. And there, in front of the Supreme Court of Virginia, amid the frippery and decadence of legal tradition, Chetta shook the hall with a massive poop explosion.

A loud *PATOOOOOOOOOOOOO* reverberated through the hall and echoed off the cavernous ceiling. A flurry of confused heads turned around in unison to see if someone had seriously just let one rip with careless abandon. Concetta had pooped so hard it had actually come out of her diaper and I saw a yellow line of slime creeping up her back. I swear it was one of the funniest moments of my life. *And that's the truth, the whole truth, and nothing but the truth, so help me God.*

Chapter 10: Potty Training

At first you have children for high

and lofty reasons. You get to sculpt a part of the next generation. You get to teach a child what it means to be a responsible, honorable, industrious person in society.

You probably also have the equally laudable goal of producing a new cadre of helpers for your house. Imagine, tiny things that you can create who will bring you a beer! Dishwashers! Oh, the possibilities.

But then they actually come out and you stop imagining what your child could do for others, and wonder if they ever will do things for themselves. Maybe, just maybe, you tell yourself ... I can get my kid to wipe her own ass.

I will summarize a newly trained child's rules for using the potty:

1. Run to potty and proudly exclaim so the neighbors can hear: "I'M POOPING!"
2. Insist on folding the toilet paper a certain way because that matters.
3. When asked to pick up your pants, explain to extremely simple mother, "I CAN'T PICK UP MY PANTS YET! FIRST I HAVE TO PICK UP

MY UNDERWEAR!"

4. Fondly bade your newfound accomplishment farewell. Explain to your mother that the pee pee and poopy is going home.

5. Spend approximately 3 hours washing hands, 2 seconds of which is actual washing and the rest admiring the bubbles at the bottom of the sink.

The really hard part of potty training is explaining that using the bathroom is a very exciting and positive thing, yet a very private and not sharable thing at that same time. Come to think of it, we are still working on it. At first, we would go into public restrooms and this would happen:

"HELLO! WHAT'S YOUR NAME?" Chloe would shout into the next stall.

The woman who just sat down in the stall next to her would mutter, "Umm..."

"I'M CLEOPATRA JOAN!" she'd reply.

The other really delicate balancing act is the art of trying to stay positive while getting awkward updates.

"The poop is coming out Mom!" she would shriek.

I'd sputter: "Oh, God, why. I mean, that's great honey! I'm so proud of you! High fives!"

Once, when we had company over, Chloe raced to the bathroom shrieking, "I HAVE TO PEE AND I HAVE TO POOP!"

"Ugh," I whimpered. "Please don't announce that to everyone."

"Okay," she corrected herself. "I HAVE TO PEE AND I DON'T HAVE TO POOP!"

Probably the funniest and simultaneously most mortifying moment was when we were at the gym and Chloe spotted a girl wearing really skimpy shorts. She pointed and shouted, "SHE'S WEARING UNDERWEAR BECAUSE SHE'S A BIG GIRL!"

Potty training Concetta was a little bit easier because she realized that her sister was out of diapers, so of course she wanted to be, too, though she wasn't quite sure how to make that happen. I first tried explaining that she had to learn to "hold it." She nodded that she understood, then grabbed her butt.

The first time we used a public restroom she broke down in tears because it had an automatic flush and she "really really really" wanted to flush it. Oh, the pain of having your bathroom glory stolen by the flourish of an automatic flush.

One day in the summer, when Chetta was mostly potty trained, she came up to me one day and shouted, "Mommy I have to go potty!"

"Okay," I said, and led her to the restroom.

"Can you help me take off my swimsuit?" she said as she tried to wriggle off her clothes. I contemplated what a pain this would be.

"Here I'll show you a little trick. You can just pull the bottom of the suit down and to the side, like this. Here I'll hold it for you. Go ahead and pee real quick," I said.

"Okay," Chetta said, hopping on the toilet. After about a minute she added, "Also, I have to poop."

At this point I was stuck. I couldn't move away without wiping her first and realized I would get a front-seat ticket to an olfactory aggravated assault.

After she was done, I helped her

clean up.

"Mom, you are the best butt wiper in the whole world," Chetta said.

"Thank you," I responded. "It's an honor I've always strived to achieve."

Chapter 11: The Art of the Remodel

Shortly after potty training Chloe, we decided to redo our bathroom. A note of caution to those courageous enough to attempt plumbing repair: you may end up spraying toilet water. In your face. But I digress.

When we moved in, the bathroom originally had a pink toilet, a pink sink and associated '60s fixtures. The walls were reminiscent of a psychedelic trip memorialized with neon sponging. Thanks to watching a little too much HGTV, we decided to remodel it ourselves.

The evolution of home repair can really be described in six easy steps:

1. I found this really easy project that would totally improve our house.
2. Okay, so maybe this is taking a bit longer than I

thought, but it's still going to look great.

3. I'm not sure how this doesn't fit perfectly since I measured it, but I'm sure it's going to be okay.
4. If I just re-jigger a few things, I'm sure it will still work.
5. Who really looks this closely at a house anyway?
6. Dear God, I hope I don't end up on ThereIFixedIt.com.

Eventually, after seven days and 12 (count 'em: TWELVE) trips to the hardware store, we were finally able to get the bathroom to both look nice and not leak. It was a feat only possible with the help of many super helpful and, I'm assuming, super bored people who were able to show us how to assemble things on YouTube.

With our downstairs bathroom out of commission, one day I heard a frantic knock on the door of my upstairs bathroom.

I had just taken all my clothes off because I was about the hop in the shower, but assuming it was an emergency, I opened the door right away and led Chloe to the toilet.

"Do you need help?" I asked, although she was way ahead of me, scurrying onto the can.

Then after sitting down, she glanced at me and asked, "Why do you have fur down there?"

"Well, because..." I began, not really sure where this would go, only to be interrupted by the most delightful cries of —

"The poop is coming out!"

"Oh, that's great honey," I said.

Did I mention this bathroom doesn't have a fan? Just a window that you can open. I oscillated between the offensively cold air rushing through the crack in the window and the offensively odorous air rushing at me from the other direction. I debated who would be scarred from this event more: the poor little girl who had just seen her mother naked or the mother about to asphyxiate and freeze simultaneously. I couldn't leave without putting my dirty clothes back on or getting my clean clothes dirty.

Finally, Chloe hopped off the toilet, sized me up with a giant grin and informed me, "Mommy, I'm potty trained!"

Chapter 12: Cleaning

I watched *The Incredibles* when it first came out over a decade ago and I thought, *Wow, it would be so cool to have super powers. I could fight crime!* I recently watched *The Incredibles* as an adult and thought, *Wow, he uses his super strength to lift the couch and she uses her stretchy power to vacuum under it! That would be convenient.*

When I wake up each day, I naively make a list in my head and think of things I want to accomplish. For some reason, I assume I may actually accomplish such things at some point. The truth is, I should probably just write "Clean up monstrous mess that has not yet occurred," since that would be more accurate.

Sometimes I get so frustrated at the slow pace of kiddie cleanup that I decide it will just be faster if I clean it up all by myself. This, of course, is a mistake because that means they will just go somewhere else and make a mess.

Once I found Chetta with the vacuum and for a fleeting second I thought she was trying to clean something on her own. Then she swung the cord and shouted, "I'M A COWGIRL!"

The other day I surveyed the tornado that exploded in my living room and declared, "Okay, it's time to clean up."

"Okay, I'll do the singing," Chloe said. "CLEAN UP! CLEAN UP! EVERYBODY EVERYWHERE..."

"No. How about you do the cleaning?" I said. That straightening up could lack an entirely musical component seemed to cause utter confusion.

"Okay, I'll watch you clean it," she said.

"Are you kidding me? No," I said, incredulous. Then, after a minute, I reconsidered and said, "Okay, I'll start, but then I need some help to clean it."

"Okay," Chloe said. "Chetta will help you."

Chapter 13: The Best Bedside Manner Ever

The newest craze seems to be *Doc McStuffins* and, though it's cheesy, I like it very much. Finally, a female lead who isn't a princess or "damsel in distress." I feel I'm incredibly qualified to be a doctor: I look great in white, I'm good at ordering people around, and I have memorized a great many Latin terms. The only thing that I wouldn't like, though, would be the sick people. That would just be depressing. Doc McStuffins gets around this conundrum by ministering solely to infirm toys, which I think is a brilliant compromise. And my kids love it.

In fact, the other day Chloe wrote out a card for Doc McStuffins.

"Ok," I said. "You can send it if you write out the address. Let me look up the address for Disney World."

Chetta, unfortunately, only heard the "Disney" part. She ran upstairs at full tilt, then rushed back down and started stripping in the middle of the kitchen.

"*I HAVE A DRESS! THE ONE FOR DISNEY WORLD! MOM I WANT TO WEAR THIS TO DISNEY WORLD.*"

McStuffins has also inspired a new love for playing doctor, though they don't quite have her bedside manner.

"MOMMY COME PLAY DOCTOR WITH ME," Chloe shouted once.

"But I haven't eaten lunch yet," I protested.

"JUST PLAY WITH ME REAL QUICK," she begged.

"Okay fine, I will be your patient just a little while."

"Okay let me take your temperature. I'm going to give you a shot. This is really going to hurt."

"Don't you mean...?"

"Now you need some medicine. This is going to taste really bad."

"You're going for honesty, I see. Wait you haven't even asked me what's wrong. My stomach hurts."

"Hmm," she said, examining my stomach with a stethoscope.

"I think it's hunger," I offered, and looked longingly at my sandwich.

"No," she said solemnly and looked up at me, as if to share a particularly grave diagnosis. "You have cavities."

Chapter 14: Poop

Before I had children, never in my wildest dreams did I imagine that one tiny person could create such a plethora of poop. Or perhaps I was just naive enough to imagine that diapers would always contain the monstrous mess.

Suddenly, the Sanitary cycle on my washer, a setting I derided as a bastion of the neurotically neat, became quite handy. I began to look at everyone I met and wonder how many diapers they had gone through in their lifetimes, and who cleaned them up. On one particularly bleach-happy day, I cleaned up after the cats, who pooped on the bathroom mat; the toddler, whose poopy diaper overflowed onto the changing table; and the bag of raw meat in the fridge, which decided to reward my meager attempts at a pork brine with a leaky bag.

Curiously, in 169 episodes, Mike Rowe never once dedicated a segment of "Dirty Jobs" to parenting — a clear oversight. Although he did do a stint as a cloth diaper cleaner and another as a monkey caretaker, so I suppose if you combine the two of them it evens out.

And then there's the dreaded "fake-out." This means you've wrestled with your young one to change her diaper, only to have to change it all over again five minutes later.

To solve this problem I have

created a nifty diaper changing flow chart:

1. *Snif f of bab y's dia per sme lls like poo p. —> Thi s is not poo p. Thi s is just fart s.*

2. *Snif f of bab y's dia per*

pro
duc
es
the
ove
rwh
elm
ing
urg
e to
pas
s
out
via
gag
refl
ex—
>
Thi
s is
poo
p.
Dia
per
acc
ordi
ngl
y.

The worst, though, is what happens

in the car seat. I don't really understand physics. Frankly, I don't know what a "physic" is. But my rather grandiose supposition is that when babies are in a small space, the velocity of the diaper explosion increases. This means up the front, up the back, all over the car seat, whatever.

The irony is that having a super duper pooper also changes your bathroom habits, too. I never in my life imagined that there would be a time when my absence for about 30 seconds would cause a deluge of tears accompanied by a high-pitched wailing and gnashing of teeth.

I solved this crapping conundrum, in a way, by instead keeping the door open. I would put the baby in a bumbo, at the edge of the bathroom, give her a toy and explain, "This is way more awkward for me than it is for you."

Then she would laugh, and then wiggle, and then in that enclosed space she would poop — all up her back.

One day we were all in the car – Hubby, Chloe, Chetta and me. We had just started a four-hour drive to go see family. We had gone approximately five blocks.

Suddenly, the whole car shook with

the rapid *pecka-pecka-pecka* of Chetta's machine-gun colon. We pulled over just as it started to pour, and I got out to go back to the baby's seat and check it out.

"What happened?" Chloe cried, craning her neck around to get a better view.

"Do you appreciate puns?" I asked.

"What?"

"Chetta just did twosies all up her onesie."

Chapter 15: "Dirty"

Occasionally, you have to go on the walk of shame. At this point in your life, that means you left the diaper bag at Target.

About a month after Concetta was born, I went to Target on Black Friday. For all the wrong reasons. If you've never seen a Diaper Genie or its equivalent, it's essentially a giant trash can that reduces diaper odors by cutting off airflow between the poopy diapers and the outside. If you've ever opened a regular diaper pail, and managed to survive the onslaught of serious sewage stink seeping into your septum, you will appreciate this. On the other hand, your precious shit stack requires special plastic rings, which are thin as a grocery bag yet expensive and hard to find. Taking stock of the situation, I realized that ironically we were in deep shit. Because we had to brave the insanity that is Target on Black Friday. Because we were out of Diaper Genie rings. Or else we would be literally in deep shit.

So newborn and toddler in tow, we slugged our sleep-deprived selves to the megamart. Within no less than five minutes, Chloe was down from the cart and wandering the aisle in search of new toys.

If I had to sum up the toddler paradox it would be this: When you're cooking, using the toilet, etc., the toddler insists on giving leg hugs or begging to be picked up. Appeals to logic or privacy are ignored. When in the store, the toddler runs for the hills and eschews all attempts to be wrangled. Getting picked up results in a rubberwoman act, followed by a successful flailing out of mommy's arms and then the keen observation that the floor of Target is "dirty."

Finally, I managed to somehow catch up with Chloe, who seemed awfully good at blending in with the crowd. I was afraid she was about to get hit with a cart.

"It's so good that you let your child be an *individual*," said a kindly older woman who was passing by in an electric cart.

"Er, yes. Thank you," I said, suddenly realizing that Chloe had on two different shoes. "Hey Chloe, why are you wearing one sock?"

"Because I couldn't find the other one," she said matter-of-factly, before turning to survey the rows of goldfish and deciding she wanted all of them. (Really, Target? *Always* an endcap of Goldfish? Ahhhh.)

That night, when we got home, we discovered two things: One, Chloe finally learned that things that fall on the floor are dirty and need to go in the trash instead of eating them. Two, if you come in from the grocery store and start putting bags on the floor because the counter is full, she will dutifully throw your groceries out.

Chapter 16: Temper Tantrums

I like how toddler temper tantrums are often called "meltdowns" because I would describe them as somewhat akin to a nuclear apocalypse. They are beyond the realm of sense and logic. It's impossible to even talk over all of the shouting. And they are never for any sane reason, such as your child is actually hurt. Instead, it seems that the normal culprit is something more like "couldn't put on *both* pink and purple pants" or "Little Mermaid's hair brush won't work."

"Mommy!" Chloe cried one day. "Are you using the potty?"

"Yes, it's fun to use the potty!" I replied, hoping that this could be a teaching moment.

"I'll wipe your butt!" she offered with enthusiasm.

"What? Absolutely not."

That was followed by an earth-shaking shriek loud enough to eviscerate my eardrums and then a torrent of tears. Because really, how could a mother be so cruel?

And then of course there is the infamous throwing of the favorite toy out of the crib. If you love your bear so much, why do you always launch him from your crib? I've never gotten a handle on this. And both my children did it repeatedly. For example:

Put baby in crib, baby screams bloody murder, check to see what's wrong, put Teddy back in crib.

Put baby in crib, baby screams bloody murder, check to see what's wrong, put Teddy back in crib.

Put baby in crib, baby screams bloody murder, try to ignore it and let her go to sleep, I can't stand it anymore, check to see what's wrong, put Teddy back in crib and TIE HIM REAL TIGHT TO THE INSIDE.

MWAHAHA I WIN.

Chapter 17: Children's books

Why would you eat green eggs and ham?
Why would you eat them, Sam-I-am?
You'd think that'd mean the eggs were old.
You'd think that'd be a sign of mold.
I'm thinking that it's just obscene
To much a bunch of old gangrene.
I'm all for trying something new,
Unless it means I'll get the flu.

I would eat them in a box,
But I don't want to get the pox.
That said we read Green Eggs and Ham
As if it were a talisman.
We go over fox and train and car.
Read it two hundred times so far.
For the love of God, just eat your food
And don't give me any attitude.

Sadly, I find many modern children's books to be evasive when it comes to plot direction. I'm always amused that most books have both an author *and* an illustrator, as if one could doodle but not come up with a simple plot line and the other could come up with a silly story but lacked the wherewithal to cartoon it out.

I imagine this prolific pair huddled around a coffee table, hatching painstaking plans to break through in the realm of children's literature.

"Yes, YES!" shouts the illustrator. "I will draw a frog on a log! I love it!"

"And I'll come up with a frog story so mundane that it will bore the bejeezus out of all those who read it!" the author adds.

"And the parents will be forced to

read it over and over and over again," says the illustrator. And then they both cackle, "MWAHAHA!" with glee.

There is a beacon of hope in the world of children's literature, though. I love the "Dr. Seuss Learning Library" books for introducing simple science. And of course, who doesn't love Seuss himself?

"I do so love green eggs and ham! Thank you! Thank you, Sam-I-am," I read to Chloe as I finished the Dr. Seuss classic just before bedtime.

"Why did he drive the car into a tree?" she asked.

"Well yes, that seems a bit silly," I said. "But look how much fun it is to try new things!"

"Why did they crash the train into the boat, though?"

"Um, yes. He does do that. Okay. But the real point is that he finally tries the food! Think how many times you decide you don't like something even though you've never eaten it. What if you never tried ice cream?"

"But aren't the green eggs and ham yucky from falling in the water?"

"Okay, I think you have me there,"

I said. "Now I'm wondering if this encourages good eating or bad driving."

And then there are fairy tales, a rather vexing cultural conundrum. On the one hand, you want your kid to know all the basics because they will see so many references throughout their lifetimes to the likes of "Little Red Riding Hood," "The Three Little Pigs," "Goldilocks and the Three Bears" and so forth. On the other hand — well, seriously, have you read any of these lately? People get beaten or eaten with stunning regularity.

"So you see," I told Chloe, the other day, "the moral of the story is to take your time and build something with a lasting foundation, so you will be protected in the future. That's why the third pig built his house out of brick," I said, pointing at the pig. I braced myself for the inevitable question about where the first two pigs went.

"But where does the pig keep his cell phone?" she said.

"Ah yes," I mused. "That would have been the better answer, I suppose. For the pig to call for help."

The next day she came up to me and shouted, "I'm gonna huff, and I'm gonna puff, and I'm gonna BLOW YOUR HOUSE DOWN!"

"Oh no!" I said. "Are you the big bad wolf?"

"NO! I'm just PRETENDING to be the big bad wolf."

My poor Cleopatra, destined to live with her incredibly simple mother.

Also, I know fairy tales are meant for imagination and fun, but part of me worries about the messages that they send.

"Do you want to hear a story about a princess, a knight and a dragon?" Chloe said to me, at about age 3.

"Sure," I said.

"Okay, once upon a time there was a princess, a knight and a dragon. And the knight dragged the princess into the tower."

"Wait, the *knight* dragged the princess into the tower? Are you sure it wasn't the dragon?"

"Hey! I'm telling the story. And then the dragon came to get her out of the tower. He was a friendly dragon. And then the princess was free! And then she went back to her mommy and daddy. And her mommy was having a baby!"

"Oh, that's very exciting," I said.

"Yes," said Chloe. "And then her mommy went to the doctor because she was having a baby. And the doctor said, 'What did the knight do to you?'"

I started laughing uncontrollably.

"Hey!" she said.

"Oh, honey, I'm not laughing at you. I'm laughing at the story. I thought it was a funny part."

"It's not a funny part! It's a story about dragons!"

"Yes of course. Please continue."

When you think about it, a library is quite a revolutionary idea. I mean, everyone is just going to share all the books? I'm pretty sure if we had no libraries before and this concept had been proposed in the present day, it would be derided as a crazy pie-in-the-sky fantasy that we will all hold hands and get along and sing kumbaya and achieve world peace through increased knowledge. And frankly, I wouldn't blame the naysayers because I'm terrible at remembering to return things on time, and I'm not quite sure why the library should trust me, either.

And yet there they stand, in every town in America, beckoning families to bring me your tired, your poor, your books that you have read 283 times, and we can switch them out for new books so you won't go insane.

The other day at the library Chloe came up to me, excited.

"Look, mom, I got this awesome book on babies!"

I sized up *Gentle Birth, Gentle Mothering: A Doctor's Guide to Natural Childbirth* with wide eyes.

"Yes... Yes, you did. I really hope this doesn't have pictures," I said.

The library is also good for inspiring reading excitement, no matter where your children are.

Recently, Chetta retreived the mail and was psyched to get a new package.

"I got a magazine!" she shouted, opening National Geographic. She opened it up and took out the junk mail card.

"AND IT COMES WITH A BOOKMARK!"

Once, before Chloe was 100% potty trained, I put her to bed, then I came back into the room about an hour later.

"Okay, sorry we forgot to put on your nighttime diaper," I said, reaching over to help put it on. "Wait a minute. The bed is wet!"

"Oh yeah, I had an ask-ka-dent," Chloe said, not looking up from her story.

"What? Wait, you just peed in your bed?!" I roared, and suddenly began tearing apart everything on the mattress, hoping it didn't yet soak in.

"Hey, you lost my page!" she wailed.

"Sorry. Mommy was just taking off all the sheets," I said.

Later, after I loaded all the clothes into the washer, she came up to me.

"I'm upset," she said.

"Oh, honey," I said, as I started to hug her. "Is it because you had an accident?"

"No," she said. "You lost my page."

Chapter 18: Children's Television

Ironically, I have Wonder Red in my head. The girl who likes to rhyme all the time. She's friends with that guy Super Why. You know. It's a TV show.

I am forever grateful for having a DVR; I'm not sure what I would do if I could not magically summon Mickey Mouse or whatnot at appropriate intervals. In fact I'm starting to wonder if they are too coddled.

"Daddy, can you fast forward through the commercials?" Chloe asked recently.

"No, sorry," said Hubby. "This movie is live."

"What does 'live' mean?" she asked, incredulous.

One day when Chloe was about 2, I shouted, "OK, naptime!'

"NO! I WANT WATCH DORA," she wailed.

So I told her why that wouldn't be possible. "Dora's sleeping. It's her naptime," I said.

There was a pause and she stared at me so long, I was beginning to think she knew I was full of crap.

"OK," she said. "We watch Sesame Street."

I'm also not sure what I would do without parental controls. When the new Ghostbusters movie came out, Chloe saw an advertisement for it and begged me nonstop to see it.

I finally had to explain that it was much too scary for a small child. After all, it was about ghosts.

Chloe sighed, shook her head, and calmly explained to me, as if she were addressing the especially simple-minded, "Mom, ghosts are just pretend."

Baby's log, supplemental:

Morning: Slept. Finally managed to secure the Cheerios box, only to discover that the Cheerios in the picture are not real. That's just cruel.

Afternoon: Slept. Discovered feet. I'm not totally sold on this socks business. They're delicious, but awfully hard to pry off your feet.

Evening: Waited until mommy opened diaper. Spit up all over. While she was distracted cleaning that up, peed all over. Hehe.

Night: Mommy read me the alphabet book. This blows my mind. You'll never guess how it ends. Later cuddled with Pandas and went to sleep. Ahh nice.

Chapter 19: Shopping with Children

I know many men who have been to war, yet the prospect of taking a child to a store scares them. Seriously.

I've also discovered that when shopping with toddlers at a megamart, all dignity is checked at the door. For example:

Okay everybody just chill in the cart while I find the list. I know there's something important we have to get. I SAID STOP SCREAMING! Thank you. Give that back to your sister and you apologize to your sister. Okay, where the hell is this list? What did we have to get again? No, I am not buying you chocolate. (Without looking up) Stop touching your sister. OK, I can't find this list, so we're just going to wing it, though I feel like there was something important on there. Here, we need conditioner. No, we're getting the conditioner in a pump, not a bottle. The only reason we're buying some more is because you dumped the whole bottle of conditioner into the tub... (Gasp) just like you dumped the whole roll of TP into the toilet! YES THAT WAS IT! TOILET PAPER! WE

NEED TOILET PAPER! Whew, that would have been terrible if we forgot that.

And of course, no matter how many times a child is implored to go to the bathroom *before* setting out, inevitably there will be a trip to a nasty restroom.

"I have to twinkle!" Chloe shouted one day from the front of the Target cart.

"What? Oh you mean tinkle?" I said.

"No, twinkle."

"Okay, I can see how that would be confusing, because of twinkle twinkle little star. But actually if you have to use the potty, it's called you have to tinkle."

"NO, TWINKLE!"

"Okay whatever, let's just go find the bathroom." I said. "No, Chetta, you can't have that. Oh, here, fine, play with it for a little bit while you sit there."

So I whirled the cart around and tried to navigate the crowded megamart with an unwieldy, poorly oiled set of wheels while simultaneously trying to avert calamity over the fight that has just broken out between the jealous toddler who decided to steal the toy and the now-screaming infant who wanted it back. It's a feat, I imagine, akin to parallel parking an aircraft carrier. It was very nearly a successful maneuver, too, when I spotted a bogey at one o'clock: Overly Friendly Lady.

Don't get me wrong. I have high aspirations to one day be an OFL. My understanding is that by a certain point in life, you can pretty much say whatever you want without repercussions. That sounds like a pretty sweet deal to me. But they have certain bits of wisdom that seem recycled at this point, and I could see this coming a mile away: the teenager speech.

"Oh honey, they're adorable," said the OFL, oblivious to the mayhem. "How old are they?"

"Three and one," I said.

"Oh yes, I remember that age. So magical. Well, enjoy it now, because when they are teenagers they will drive you crazy."

Here's what I wanted to say: *Look lady. Last night, your teenager slept through the night. The whole night. She may have slept in even. Then she got up, washed herself, dressed herself and fed herself. And the most exciting part of it all? She wiped her OWN ass. I'm sure you are worried about her running around, causing you stress, and the boys running around trying to get her pregnant. Because then she will have kid/cart craziness issues, too. Yes, I know having a teenager is a difficult thing. But that doesn't mean you can go around telling mothers of small children how easy it is for them while they are out shopping for shit stack liners.*

But, I didn't tell her that, obviously. I wussed out and thanked her sweetly and headed to the public restroom so that tiny hands could touch every dirty surface despite my consternation.

Chapter 20: Confusing Adult Rules

As soon as Chloe learned how to talk, she kept running up to the cats and screaming, "MEOW!" Then she got all confused when they ran away, like, "hey, I'm speaking your language, dummy."

When you think about it, the world is a complex place filled with many confusing adult rules, particularly if you are in the toddler set. I had never contemplated the extent of such conundrums until I had children. For example: Yes, your cat loves you. No, you may not kiss the cat on the mouth. I want you to throw, but only a ball and only outside. If you drop your food on the floor, it's dirty. We have to throw it out. Just because your toys are on the floor does not make them dirty. Why did you throw them out?

I'll describe for you a typical day:

"Would you like some hash browns for breakfast?" I said.

Chloe's face lit up.

"Hash BROWNIES?!" she said.

"No, hash BROWNS."

"BROWNIES?"

"No, hash BROWNS."

Chloe then looked in the toaster, and her face fell.

"These are just potatoes!"

Later, while playing in the neighbor's backyard:

"I hear a siren! It's a police car!" Chloe cried.

"Yes," I said. "They're going to fight crime."

"Yeah," Chloe said. "They're going to fight crying."

Later at home, she's confused because she added "PLEASE!" to her repeated requests of "COME HERE KITTY," but sadly the cat ignored her.

Then, at the doctor for her checkup, Chloe spied the aquarium.

"It's a fishy!" she cried with glee and started pointing to the aquarium.

"No," said the little boy beside her. "It's a bumblebee."

"NO, IT'S A FISHY!" Chloe cried, hysterical, and started getting up in the little boy's face.

I tried to stay calm.

"Please don't yell at him," I said.

Chloe still got up in his face, started shaking a finger at him, but dutifully told him in a whisper: "IT'S A FISHY!"

Later, before dinner, Chloe helped me set the table.

"I need a roller coaster," she said.

"Really?" I mused.

"For under my milk."

"What? Oh, okay. Honey, that's just a... Well, whatever. Here you go." I said, handing her a coaster.

Then, while eating dinner, I told her, "Okay, you have to eat your meat. You need protein to grow big and strong."

Then she got really confused. "But I am a big girl!"

"Well yes, you are, but..."

"I poop on the potty!"

"Yes, and I'm very proud of you, but protein will make you... an even bigger girl, I guess. Just eat it."

Chapter 21: Chloe's Preschool

"What did you play today?" I said while picking Chloe up from school.

"We played doctor. I played doctor with Jason!"

Hmm, maybe I don't like this Jason after all. I mean, playing doctor with my daughter? Whoa whoa whoa, what does that mean? And he wears black nearly every day. What's up with that? That can't be a normal thing. I mean, sure, it's his favorite Batman shirt. Or maybe he's just trying to be a hipster. And he's much older. I mean, he's already 4. That's borderline scandalous. Jason, I'm onto you son. Er, well whenever you learn to read, you'll be reading this and know that I'm onto you. So there.

Chloe loved preschool more than anything. Early on she would run right in while I stammered something like, "Okay good..." I thought my dropping her off wouldn't embarrass her until at least high school or maybe middle school. But clearly, I was wrong.

The number one thing she always wanted to tell me about preschool was about snack. The second thing she liked to tell me about is the jobs.

"I got to be line leader today! And Anna got to be snack helper number one!" Chloe roared one day, as I picked her up from preschool.

Aha, so this must be the source of Miss Marjorie's power, I thought. You give a kid a chore, but tell the kid that it's a special honor. Yeah, I could do that.

"Hmm, who should I pick to be table setter number one?" I asked that night, right before dinner. Chloe looked up at me as I walked into the living room holding Chetta.

"Hmm. Such a tough choice. Maybe I should pick Chetta. That would be so much fun, wouldn't it, Chetta?"

"Yeah, you pick Chetta," said Chloe, going back to her puzzle.

Crap, she called my bluff, I thought. Well, now I have to play it up.

"Come on Chetta you can set the table," I said. "Here, why don't you hold...

no don't hold the knife... here you take a spoon... OW! CHETTA! You just whacked me in the face with the spoon! Okay that's enough of this."

Preschool has gotten so intense since I was a kid. There's counting, art, music, even science. They did an experiment in science that I did in college. I'm not sure yet if that is a big win for my preschool or a big fail for my college. And they are constantly having some sort of party in preschool, from what I've gathered.

"What is Cleopatrick's day?" Chloe asked me once when I picked her up from school.

"Oh, honey, you dressed up in green today at preschool for St. Patrick's Day," I explained.

"No, Cleopatrick's day," she corrected me.

"No, just St. Patrick."

"CLEOPATRICK!"

I just sighed and gave up at that point.

Another time, in November, I picked her up from school and she told me that Mary had a baby.

"Are you sure?" I asked. "I think it's

'Mary had a little lamb'."

"Mary had a baby!"

"No honey, she had a little lamb."

"SHE HAD A BABY! And she named him Jesus."

"Oh. No, you're right, actually she did."

At the end of the year came the biggest celebration of all: the multicultural day. Each family was to bring a cultural dish and the kids would sing a song and do a dance. I brought pasta with meatballs and we eagerly waited for Chloe's turn to go up with her group.

Finally, we got our cameras ready as the 2-day kids got up to sing. And there was my kid: the littlest one, with absolutely no idea what was going on. Note to self: Sign this kid up for the Simon Says team.

Chapter 22: The "Why" Phase

At some point, they all come up with three little letters are so relentless: why.

At first, I welcomed it as adorable. Clearly, Chloe was broadening her intellectual horizons and starting to put things together into a sensible framework, I mused. But when you're reading a book and are asked "Why" approximately 53 times, it gets to you.

I tried saying, "I don't know." But then she would answer back with an "OH YOU KNOW!" that's simultaneously flattering, since she thinks I possess all knowledge in the world, and exasperating because really it never occurred to me if the world would ever stop turning. (Actually, it is slowing down very, very slowly. I had to look that one up.)

Once, while working with Chloe on her Spanish workbook, we came across the word "mal," meaning bad, and a picture of a girl holding her stomach.

"See this girl has a stomach ache. That is muy mal," I said.

"Why does she have a stomach ache?" Chloe asked.

"Um, because she ate some bad chicken."

"Why?"

"Because it was undercooked."

"Why?"

"Because she didn't cook it long enough."

"Why?"

"Because she didn't put a meat thermometer in."

"Why?"

"Because the meat thermometer was broken."

"Why?"

"Because it fell."

"Why?"

"Because she dropped it."

Then suddenly Hubby interjected, "You're going to have to remember all your B.S."

Yes, that's probably true.

I've found that, ironically, parents seem to slip back into using "why," though the motivation is much different. Such as "WHY did you STEP INTO THE GIANT MESS OF FLOUR on the countertop to get a plate?"; "WHY, WHY did you give yourself bangs?"; and upon discovering a whole tub of soap dumped on the floor, "WHY WHY WHY was this a good idea?"

Of course the "why" phase also means that your young one is looking for a logical explanation for things, which can be helpful sometimes.

I was struggling one day while trying to dress Chetta on the bed, while simultaneously trying to fend off Chloe, who alternated between jumping on the bed and trying to steal Chetta's toy.

"I told you three times not to do that, Chloe! Jesus!" I shouted. She got quiet. "Why Jesus?"

"Because... um... Jesus... would want you to share. Obviously. Now let her have the toy while I dress her then you can take turns."

Chapter 23: Going to Bed

Once Chloe yelled from her bedroom that she couldn't go to sleep because there were monsters. So I did what any self-respecting mother would do. I assured her that monsters were very real, but if she stayed very, very still they wouldn't get her. Because monsters can only see things that move.

I've summarized successful bedtime strategies into the following chart:

"Okay, bedtime!" —> *Does not work.*

"Okay, let's go upstairs." —> *Does not work.*

"Let's go read a story upstairs." —

> Does not work.

"There's monsters upstairs! Should we go up and poof them away?" —> Instant excitement, running upstairs, followed by screams of "POOF!"

I don't pretend to understand the toddler psyche, but I do hope to use it to my advantage.

Getting them into bed, though, is only half the battle. Getting them to go to sleep is another. For example, once when visiting my parents, I put Chloe down to sleep in the guest room. I thought, *gee, I don't hear anything on the monitor. Perhaps my little angel has fallen asleep quickly.* False. A bedroom check reveals a foiled diaper cream plot. White gunk is wiped off of hands, bed and Teddy. An hour passes. *Surely my cherub has succumbed to the sandman.* False. Bedroom check reveals no toddler in bed. Uh oh. Future gymnast has surmounted the nearby big bed. This is one of the main reasons we eventually got a video monitor.

Another time, I couldn't find Chloe on the video monitor, so I went in her room. I was expecting to find her playing in the closet or something, but was completely surprised when I opened the door and there she was staring right back at me, almost at eye level.

It took me a second to actually process what had happened. She had snuck out of bed and opened the drawers to her bureau. Then, using the drawers as a foothold, she had climbed to the top of her dresser. There she had found a tub of moisturizer and proceeded to slime her dresser and herself with it. (Have I mentioned this kid likes to smell pretty?)

It took me a while to de-gunk the dresser and the toddler, but finally I was able to escort *Cleopatra Joan: Escape Artist, Mountain Climber, Moisturizer Fan* back to bed.

Chetta, being a night owl, is even worse. One night I heard a giant THUMP. I went upstairs to investigate. When I got to her room, I found a lamp on the floor. And two tiny hands holding up covers way over her head thinking she was invisible.

Another time, I went to check on her at 11 p.m. The light was on and she was hiding behind *Cloudy With a Chance of Meatballs* trying to stay statuary still. I love that 2-year-olds think they're *real* slick.

Now, granted, I am a night owl,

too. Morning is not my forte, and I'm pretty sure I've never said anything nice to anyone between the hours of 1 and 6 a.m. Hubby disputed this once, and I thought he was going to say that I *had* said something nice to someone in the wee hours of the morning. He actually wanted to correct the hours to between 1 and 8 a.m.

Chloe, on the other hand, will wake up early on a weekend, come down to our room and attempt to talk to me. I will, in turn, attempt coherent conversation, then I will make a concerted effort to get up and probably fall back to sleep. Usually, this ends with me rising later only to discover I have authorized Cheez-Its for breakfast or something.

But putting a night owl to bed is exasperating. Once, after putting Chetta back into her room for the 314th time, I locked her in there. Hearing nothing on the monitor for a bit, I congratulated myself on finding a novel way to get her to sleep. When I went to check on her at 10 p.m., though, I found the light on and a tiny blond head behind *One Fish, Two Fish, Red Fish, Blue Fish.* Apparently this one has a little star, and this one has a little car, and this one is too clever by far.

Chapter 24: Little Parrots

Accidentally drop sippy cup under car. Dammit.

Accidentally teach toddler new word. Darn it.

My children will probably be sailors. Not because Hubby was in the Navy, but because of the amount of times I have accidentally cursed in front of them.

I keep forgetting that they are absorbing everything I say and preparing to parrot it back at an inopportune moment. For example, I think Chloe has picked up the habit of sighing and saying, "some people just don't know how to drive" while we're sitting in traffic. She has also taken to calling out to each unhelmeted biker, "idiot!" as we drive past.

I really thought I had caused trouble when I accidentally said "HOT DAMN!" but, thankfully, she looked at me and said, "NO, mom! It's not hot damn. It's hot DOG!"

Once while we were up visiting my

parents, I helped her wash her hands after using the toilet. Chloe was fascinated by the bathroom.

"Why do Nona and Grandad have two sinks?" she asked.

"Uh yeah," I said. "Well, some people have two sinks in case they want to use both at the same time. Okay, you're all done now, let's go."

A few days later, while washing her hands, Chloe proudly exclaimed, in front of family, "See, Nona and Grandad go pee pee together and then they use both sinks!"

Chapter 25: Sick Kids

The Mucinex commercials are always horrifying to me and here's why: Some twisted soul decided their mascot should be mucus. How did that go down? Some pharmaceutical executives were all sitting around at the table and one of them said, "You know what's fun? Phlegm." And someone else agreed? What advertising ideas did they reject?

It's not just people in snot suits, either. It is actual computer-generated goo, which means an animation company has to spend hours and hours properly programming the pestilence. Some poor coder has to sit at a console and think: What is the proper spotlighting for slime? Should the snot saunter or jiggle?

I imagine said programmer at a bar somewhere, kicking back after a long day of animating abhorrence, nursing a glass of beer. A potential date comes up to the bar and tries to strike up some small talk with this sad soul.

"So, what do you do for a living?" the stranger asks.

The programmer answers honestly, "I make boogers come to life!"

The questioner thinks this must be some sort of misunderstanding.

"Um, so you animate the boogey-man? Are you part of some horror show production?"

"No," says the programmer, looking away wistfully. "*Actual* boogers."

The potential date backs away slowly.

According to my baby book, during the winter it's normal for kids to have a cold every other week. I feel like I always seem to have an "above average" winter. I guess the most frustrating thing is not that they're sick, but that you can't really give them anything besides pain medicine, which of course won't help their coughing and snotting. (A few years back the FDA banned cold medicine for children under 4.)

When kids turn 2, though, pharmacies do have some homeopathic medicine for coughing. "Homeopathic" is a Greek term for "sugar water that you will buy and tell your child it will make them feel better."

Once, when I was pregnant with Chetta, I was down and out with a bad cold. Chloe took a tissue out of the box, crumpled it up and smushed me in the face with it. I hardly had time to squeal when she took it off and then put it back in the box. So helpful.

Chetta seems to have learned from her sister. Once, while having a bad cold, she got ahold of a tissue box. I was going to stop her, but it was so darn cute — she took a tissue out of the box and covered her nose with it while making scrunchy faces. Then she threw the tissue on the ground. Then she took the next tissue, gave herself a facewash, and threw it away. She emptied the whole box like that.

The worst, though, is when they have a fever. And... sometimes even if they don't. The other day, I took Chloe's temperature orally and good news — she did not have a fever. The bad news: I realized afterward that I accidentally used the rectal thermometer.

Chapter 26: Ashes, Ashes, We All Fall Down

Our church in Virginia had a crying room. Or as a friend of mine liked to call it, the first realm of purgatory.

Believe it or not, though, getting caught in the cacophony of clamorous kiddies in the crying room is a bit of stress relief. It's better than waiting until your own bundle of joy's inevitable freak-out and having to pick her up and take her out of the church. Everyone's a Christian until your child is giving her own rendition of shouting Hallelujah and just won't stop as you make a less-than-graceful exit.

The kids probably didn't get as much from it as they would in the regular church, but then I think they were a little too young to understand existential things anyway. Believe me, I tried.

"Today, is a special day. It's Ash Wednesday. We're going to get ashes," I said one day when Chloe was about 3.

"YEAH! And we can be astronauts, and we can say BLASTOFF!" Chloe said.

"No, ashes and astronauts aren't related. Ashes are like what's left over after something burns."

"You *burnt* something? In the oven?"

"No. No, the ashes are like a symbol, that Easter is coming. Easter is when Jesus died and rose from the dead."

"Like the green marker?"

"Yes, I guess I did say the green marker died after you left the cap off and it dried out. Uh, well that might not be coming back..."

Chapter 27: Sports

Like any good middle-class American parent, I have high hopes of my kid going to college someday. Which is why I put them in sports early. How else will we afford it?

We started in gymnastics, and Chloe loved it. On the first day, she was the most eager one, walking up to the teacher to announce, "MINE NAME CHLOE! I'M READY TO GO NOW!"

Also, Chloe loves watching hockey. She particularly likes the part with the goals. "HUGS! HUGS!" She shouts. She is still too small to actually play hockey, but this has not stopped her becoming an expert in it.

"So mommy played hockey last night," I said one morning after I had played a game late the night before.

"Oh yeah! I saw you on TV!" Chloe said.

"Uh... Maybe not. But I scored a goal!"

"Did you score three goals?"

"Uh... No, remember I scored one. But that's still good."

"Oh. Well, I played hockey last night, too."

"Really? How did you do that?"

"Because I really wanted to."

"Uh... hmmm."

"Yeah, and I scored TEN goals."

"Really?"

"Yeah. And a hat trick."

"Oh, that's quite impressive."

Chapter 28: Teaching Letters and Numbers

Around the Christmas season, as I was going through the mail, I noticed something addressed to Chloe.

"Oh, look! Your friend Sam sent you a letter," I said.

"YEAH!" She said. "Is it the letter C? I hope it's letter C!"

One of the great things about having little kids is that you get to be their first teachers. The downside is you have to explain something as complex and irregular as the English language to a person with no ability to relate.

For example, once Chloe asked, "What sound does Y make?"

"It makes a 'ya' sound," I told her. "Like 'ya ya ya yes.' "

"No!" She shouted. "It makes a 'wa' sound! 'Wa wa wa why!' "

"Okay, well I can see how that would be confusing, but actually the letter that makes a 'wa' sound is W."

"No, Y!"

"No, W."

"You're being a bad girl," she said.

"You're not listening to me."

Chapter 29: That Darling Moment When Your Little Girl Hands You a Bag of Penises

I'm a little nervous about having a boy soon. Because up until now, I could yell, "BE NICE TO YOUR SISTER!" without having to turn around to the back seat.

Traveling with kids is the art of coordinating nap time, traffic patterns and chow time into one fell swoop. And if you own a sedan, packing is a test of your geometry skills as well. Even the best made plans, though, cannot account for traffic jams, flight delays and child sleep disturbances. Tiny creatures with no attention span in tiny spaces, what could go wrong?

While in Virginia, we decided to drive to Ohio to visit Hubby's family, usually about an eight-hour trek. We had a grand plan: We would leave at 6 p.m. and get in at 2 a.m. Brutal for the driver, but the kids would be asleep most of the time, no problem.

So we were off and sure enough

they were asleep according to plan. At 2 a.m., we finally rolled in there completely exhausted. Okay, confession: I conked out at the end while Hubby drove. But the kids had slept most of the way, so I chalked the night up to a total win.

By 2:30 a.m., everyone finally crawled into bed, asleep. I had just dozed off when Chloe tapped me on the shoulder.

"I have to use the potty," she said.

So I took her to the bathroom. Coming back to bed, and exhausted, she had a temper tantrum. For about a half-hour straight, she let out a stress-inducing scream, I'm guessing because she was so confused and tired out of her mind. Or who knows what really, I have to admit I was quite out of it too at that point.

By 3:30 a.m., I had finally, finally gotten back to sleep again when I got another tap on the shoulder.

"I have to use the potty," Chloe said.

I whimpered feebly and got her back to the toilet. There was a long awkward moment before I realized she didn't actually have to go. This time *I* had a tantrum.

The next day, I put both kids down to sleep in the same room, and in record time they were very quiet.

About a half-hour later, Unsuspecting Relative asked, "Don't you want to go check on them?"

"Oh, no," I said. "They were up for half the night last night, so they both probably zonked out."

Quite some time passed by and at about 10 p.m. Chloe came out of the room all smiles. She walked up to me and handed me a bag of candy.

"Can you open this? Can I have some?" she asked.

I looked down. It was penis candy. Oh dear God.

As it turns out, Unsuspecting Relative had gotten several gag gifts at her bachelorette party and had put them all in a box, having never used them. She put the box on a low shelf and later forgot about it.

I walked backed to the room and creaked open the door. Chetta was sleeping down in the pack-in-play and a box of knick-knacks lay open on the bed. A white substance had been spread all over the room. The air smelled heavily of flowers and lavender.

Inside the box on the bed, a tub of "Pure Seduction" moisturizer lay open. There was white goo on the bed. And the floor. And the fan. And Chloe's pajamas.

I peered over into the pack-n-play and saw Chetta happily snoozing away. She must have slept the whole time her sister graciously endowed her with gobs of flowery lotion.

"What... is... this...?" I stammered.

"Doesn't it smell pretty!" Chloe said.

Part III: Oklahoma

Chapter 30: Every Night, My Honey Lamb and I

After two years in finance, Hubby decided he really hated it and wanted to go back to engineering, like he did in the Navy. A chemical company recruited him and he asked them to fly me out for his interview, too, because a big part of him taking a job would be convincing his wife, he said.

We arrived in Oklahoma City late at night, and finally got a rental car at about 10:30 p.m. It was past midnight when we approached the town of Enid for the first time. The skies had opened up and a pounding rain battered our little rental car that could. The windshield wipers had been turned up to "insanity," but still they couldn't shovel water off fast enough. An unfortunate turtle expired when it tried to cross the road and we couldn't see it in time.

The next day, Hubby went off for his interview and said I should drive around to check out the town. I said that sounded like a great idea. Then I got back to the hotel and I went straight back to sleep because with two small children you are always sleep-deprived and who would seriously move to Enid, anyway?

In the end, though, I understood him wanting to pursue his passion and with a lower cost of living, I could eventually go back to journalism, too. I now work mostly as a legal reporter, which is essentially the task of documenting the various ways the Oklahoma justice system tries to out-crazy Texas.

Oklahoma is now the seventh state I've lived in, and I'm often asked where the best place to be is. That question is hard to answer, of course, because there are aspects of every place I've been that simultaneously make me miss it and appreciate that I'm not there.

If I could have, say, the beaches of South Carolina, the cheesesteaks of Philly, the tacos of San Diego, the museums in D.C., the amenities of Northern Virginia, the hockey in Rochester and the lack of traffic in Oklahoma, then I would be very happy indeed.

On the other hand, I could do without the cockroaches in South Carolina, the bitter cold of Rochester, the remoteness of Oklahoma and the traffic/expense of living in California, Virginia, Pennsylvania or D.C.

Instead of finding the "best" place to live, I think it's more likely that Hubby and I will lose all our friends. Because when someone says "It's cold," I have to shout, "HA! You think this is cold? When I was in Rochester..." Or "Did you feel that earthquake?" and I respond, "HA! You think that was an earthquake? When I lived in California..." And really, who can stand such insufferable story-toppers.

Probably the biggest difference

between Oklahoma and most other places is the wind. It is relentless and powerful, a constant rushing force that surrounds you, swirls your hair in all directions, and scatters every paper in your hand down the street.

The wind has enough force to push your heavy trash can into your neighbor's yard, and yet this is the weak wind, the kind that doesn't swirl around and kill you.

Cool dry air from over the Rockies combines with warm air from the Gulf of Mexico, giving incredible strength to the storms and putting most of Oklahoma in the angry red part of Tornado Alley, at least, according to the National Weather Service map.

The result of this mishmash, though, is that few days are simply grey; most are either bright and sunny or it's raining so hard that it's hailing.

And the wind actually feels nice, particularly on hot days, and also because it has the added effect of keeping off the bugs. Well, the little bugs at least. I'm fairly certain the whole neighborhood got a show the other day when I screamed, ran into the driveway, ripped off my shirt, and shook it like a bullfighter at a martini-making contest. But thanks to an enormous cricket that would not get off my back, I am now super prepared if I ever win a World Cup.

Counterintuitively, winter is more difficult in the state than summer is, because when it's 104 degrees, a brisk wind feels very good, whereas, when it's 30 degrees, a 25mph wind is just chilling to the bone.

The economy is also much different. Twenty percent of Oklahoma GDP comes from the oil industry, or at least did before the latest slump. Everywhere else I've been, the media constantly laments that gas prices are too high whereas now they only complain that gas prices are too low.

Even in front of the Oklahoma Capitol Building, a glistening white monument of neoclassical architecture, you can see a giant oil derrick. Oklahomans are a practical people.

There's a small museum in Enid that I highly recommend, the Cherokee Strip Regional Heritage Center. It's fairly new and does a good job of mixing informative history, interactive displays and artifact presentation.

If you don't get the opportunity to see it, though, I would summarize Northern Oklahoma history as follows: The U.S. government first designated it Indian Territory, forcibly marching dozens of tribes here in the famous Trail of Tears beginning in the 1830s. Years later, the government needed more land for settlers and so they again gave Native Americans short shrift, opening up 6 million acres – the biggest land run in U.S. history.

Those settlers scored free homesteads, but let's face it, life was still tough for them. They obtained farms in an area previously thought of as marginal land, in an era before the advent of air conditioning, in summers that routinely reach 102 degrees.

In a strange way, I think the settlers and the Native Americans had a lot in common. Oklahoma was not their first choice, but they made it work. In a country that is now sadly only 1 percent[4]

---

[4] Pureblood, that is. Every tribe defines membership in different ways, and most only require a Native American ancestor. But the point

Native American, their cultural centers, mostly in Oklahoma, have helped to preserve tribal languages and customs. And the settlers made Oklahoma one of the top wheat producers in the U.S. I don't know about you, but bread and butter is my, well, bread and butter.

Enid, Oklahoma, is a small town of about 50,000 people located approximately two hours north of Oklahoma City and two hours west of Tulsa. For its size, the city has produced some remarkably productive people. It was the hometown of two double Pulitzer Prize winners, a star opera singer, a Medal of Honor winner, the current lieutenant governor, and an astronaut. For reasons I can't seem to grasp, though, the welcome sign on the way into town says "Enid: Home of Kaci Hundley, Miss Oklahoma 2001." *A long time ago, someone here was very pretty.*

We moved to Enid in July 2014. Hubby and I took about three days to drive the 1,300 miles in his Honda Civic, from Virginia down through North

---

here isn't the exact number, but that the remaining population is unfortunately much smaller.

Carolina, Tennessee, Arkansas and, finally, into Oklahoma. We stopped in Oklahoma City, so I could take the bar exam. This time, instead of studying, I just wrote "it depends," which of course is the correct legal answer for everything. I passed.

"Mom, what did you want to be when you were little?" Chloe asked one day.

"Well," I thought about it for a moment. "Honestly, probably a hockey player."

"WOW! You are three things! A hockey player, a mommy and a lawyer."

"Yes, I suppose."

"When I grow up, I want to be three things too — a mommy, a geologist and a cowgirl."

"That sounds pretty awesome. That sounds like a very Oklahoma thing to do."

"When I grow up I want to be just like you, mom."

"I'm writing all this down for your teenage years."

"I REALLY want to be a geologist. And a mommy. I'll go pick out big rocks and leave them outside your house as a present. I'll leave you a note so you know it's from me," she explained.

"If I get a large rock as a present, I'll know it's from a geologist, no note required," I said.

Oklahoma is a nice safe place to raise kids, though I'm starting to wonder if they're even a bit *too* sheltered. For example, the other day Chloe thought the idea of the earth being mostly ocean was just stupid.

Once we traveled about an hour outside of Enid to visit a corn maze. As soon as we got out of the car, Chloe stared at the ground in wonder and shrieked with delight.

"Look the world is turning over right here!" Then she confidently added, as if explaining to me complicated science, "It's because of the earth's rotation."

"No, honey," I said, gently. "We just parked on a hill."

Chapter 31: Why I read E-books

Shopping for a book before having children:
**

You grab a coat and stop to select a cute fall scarf before hopping into the car. All of this takes 30 seconds.

You arrive at the bookstore and pause to marvel at the front entrance at the cornucopia of wonder that awaits you. You take a breath of the fresh air and stare in awe at the tables of brightly-colored stacks surrounding you: literature, history, biography, travel. The secrets of the universe just waiting to be opened and loved by you. You take your time and consider each in turn, finally choosing an interesting one but secretly whispering to the other contenders that you will be back again soon.

You order a latte at the little cafe in the store and start reading your new book. It transports you like an oversized stalk into a world of giant new ideas. You sip lovingly on your cup of magic beans. You contemplate the mysteries of life: love, loss, joy.
**

Shopping for a book after having children:
**

You begin the process of sorting children, coats, mittens, hats, socks, shoes. After 20 minutes and getting asked 400 times, one child still does not have a shoe on. No one can find a full pair of mittens. Where was the last place you had the mittens? You know what? JUST WEAR THE MISMATCHED MITTENS. No one cares. You finally get in the car. You struggle with the car seat because someone is sitting on the buckle and it's nearly impossible to fish it out. Finally, everyone is strapped in LIKE THEY'RE GOING TO THE MOON.

You arrive at the bookstore after what seems like an eternity because the whole time you listened to the cacophony of Child A singing enthusiastically and off key while Child B whined about the singing and begged her sister to stop it.

You spend about 10 seconds trying to find a book before the first crisis. This crisis is always extremely important, such as "she called me a do-do-head" or "I just realized I have this cut that's not even bleeding and I need a Band-Aid RIGHT NOW."
You finally defuse the crisis and get to spend another 10 seconds trying to choose a book. Then your child begs you to read Curious George. And again. And again.

Spoiler alert: George will sneak away and cause trouble, but the man in the yellow hat will somehow make it all right in the end. And again. And again. And again.

You spend about another 10 seconds again trying to pick out a book before Child A, who swore she did not need to go potty, suddenly has to do so or else. You take both into the bathroom and explain to Child B that she is not to touch ANYTHING. She nods, folds her hands together and bounces around for a bit, eagerly trying to restrain herself. She succeeds for approximately one minute. Then, intensely curious, she breaks and decides to investigate the trash can. THE TRASH CAN. THE **DIRTIEST** THING in a public bathroom, which is the dirtiest room in the whole store. Now *you* have a crisis, and hands are thoroughly scrubbed all around.

You spend another 10 seconds trying to pick out a book when both children decide they are famished and just can't make it anymore. You give up and go home to fix dinner. While waiting for various things to cook, you finally have five minutes with which you can download a book to your phone.

The next day at the park, you start reading your book, in the five minutes you have before someone will beg you to push them on a swing. You start to contemplate the mysteries of the universe, like how all people can be sorted into those who have small children and those who do not. You start to think of all the people you see in the park and wonder, if you put all the diapers they ever used into one big stack, just how big would that pile be?

A smug stranger approaches you in the park and sees you reading a book, three characters at a time, on your phone. She tells you she is at the park with her niece and nephew, which you had figured anyway since she has hair she actually had time to blow dry and – dear God — she's wearing a coordinating set of scarf and mittens. You grumble incoherently and hope she goes away.

She presses on, explaining that she would love to read e-books, but she really can't because she just loves the feel of a book in her hand. And you open your mouth to start on a long explanation. You're about to say how you love the feel of real books, too, and literature and coffee houses and learning, but frankly right now you'd be happy just to poop on your own with no company or perhaps get through an entire shower without a small person opening the door to let all the cold air in and tattle on her sister. But before you can do that, said small person starts wailing because the little boy in the park wants to play basketball and doesn't want to play with her, which she can't understand because doesn't everybody want to play "family"? She even offered to let him be the daddy! And so, without ever really finishing the conversation, you go to console your child on the mystery that is boys.

Chapter 32: Working Out

I've discovered this delightful place, the YMCA, where they will take your children every day if you are a member. For an additional fee, they will take your kids swimming while you lounge in the hot tub. This is called "swimming lessons" and, as an additional bonus, they even teach the children how to swim so that you, of course, can spend future sessions lounging in the hot tub while they play in the pool. The hot tub is rather large and even has massaging whirlpool jets, so we can all agree it's worth the additional dollars.

The downside, of course, of going to the gym is that you'll end up surrounded by incredibly fit people who will remind you that you should probably be a little more active. Don't get me wrong, I am incredibly healthy. After all, I mix my rum with Vitamin Water.

But about a year after having Chloe, I realized somewhat disappointingly that I was still in fat pants. And so came the choice: slim down or buy a whole new wardrobe.

I couldn't really buy new pants, though, because as we've already established I spend entirely too much on mommy hot tub time, so that pretty much left the slim down option.

I started Weight Watchers, which worked delightfully well for me, though measuring everything was painful. The diet works sort of like this: The amount of fat in one doughnut is the equivalent to the amount of fat in 70 oranges. And let's face it; you couldn't have that many oranges if you tried. I also did Weight

Watchers after having Chetta and lost a lot of weight, and one more time rather recently, this one not induced by a baby but perhaps a misestimation of the proper rum-to-Vitamin-Water ratio.

So I went to the gym one day recently and dropped off the kids in the kiddie area while I went to tackle the elliptical.

It's a rather fun machine, and there are little sensors that light up to identify the muscles you are using depending on which way you are heading, and how high you have set the hill. So the next day, when you have pulled a muscle, you can say, in a matter-of-fact tone, "Sadly, I overstrained my glutes at the gym," which sounds a lot more serious than "my ass hurts because I'm out of shape."

After a few minutes on the elliptical, I was a little more winded than I should have been, or at least was before I had a baby. I spied an old woman out of the corner of my eye and decided to keep pace with her because surely I could outrun an old woman.

She easily outpaced me, of course, the overachiever, but I kept going so that I could at least keep my dignity somewhat intact.

After working out, I took a long shower. You'd probably think that a shower in a Spartan setting the equivalent of a public restroom would be horrible. On the contrary, it was delightful. You can actually take your time without small children screaming the entire time or opening the door to let all the cold air in and announce important things like "she called me a hippo butt."

I was feeling a little guilty for taking so long in the bathroom, both in terms of water wasted and time away from my children, when I went to pick them up.

"Ugh, Mom, why can't you work out more?" Concetta said. "We were right at the end of Scooby Doo."

"I'm... sorry?" I said.

When we got home, we had hamburgers on the grill. Everyone else had chips with their burger, while I had carrots.

I used a little food scale to measure the amount of hamburger I could eat, as well as bread.

"How is the drug business going?" Hubby chuckled while he observed my science experiment.

"You're hilarious," I replied, adding on an extra few ounces of cheese and weighing it on the tiny scale. "You know, this is a lot easier than calculating food by volume."

Then my plate was looking a little sad, so I put some more carrots on the plate, and some more carrots. And then some more carrots.

"I think you're taking this a little too far," he said as I started pouring my wine.

"Don't be silly," I said, as I crouched down to look at the measuring cup from the proper angle, so that I could get an accurate reading of the meniscus of the wine. Yes, all those years of science, and this is the first time that knowing what a "meniscus" is has actually helped me.

"There's no way you need to be so crazy about this. If you worked out and ate healthy, I'm sure it'd be fine," he said.

"Ugh, this is me eating healthy," I retorted as we finally sat down.

Outside the window, I spied a rabbit who was suspiciously eyeing my carrots. It glared at me. I glared back at it. Our eyes locked in a Wild West

Showdown over beta carotene.

I'm just kidding, I didn't really see a rabbit. All of the rabbits in the area have since starved from lack of carrots.

Chapter 33: Cooking with Children

Let's talk for a second about food, and how it keeps lying to you.

"Wild Mountain Blueberries" — The harvesters braved the danger and unpredictability of *"The Wild,"* but somehow managed to survive and bring back these delicious blueberries.

"Black Forest Ham" — The sellers ventured into a dark and scary forest to bring back the wild boar they found roaming around in the foliage.

"Artisan" anything — This wasn't packed by an underpaid immigrant. A group of artists created this while contemplating how to make your meal more beautiful and creative.

"Sundried tomatoes" — Oh no, they weren't actually dried in a commercial food dehydrator, the tomatoes laid out in the Tuscan sun. Everyone sat around, drinking wine and watching the sunset as the they perfectly shriveled and no bugs or bacteria got to them.

"Italian Seasoning" — Actually, this one is real. They chop up tiny Italians. We can't help that we're delicious.

Probably my favorite food lie, though, is the Taco Bell commercial where the boy busts out some intricate Parkour moves while simultaneously munching on his crazy cheesy crunchy creation. I think the point of the commercial is to imply that you, too, could be incredibly cool like this kid, if only your lunch were all wrapped up in a tortilla and easily portable. In reality, it's actually designed for shoving calories into your face while handling the two tons of steel and rubber you insist upon for all locomotion. But yes, in theory you could eat your burrito thingy while embarking on excellent adventures.

The pretentiousness of food has reached incredible heights, particularly on the Food Network. This happens at least once on every sort of contest show: A line of judges stares in silent admiration as a chef reveals a rainbow plate of chopped up little bits. The chef nods confidently and says, "I have for you here a deconstructed [*fancy dish*]..." I scream at the TV, "You moron, that's just a toddler lunch!"

I've discovered toddler lunches are a necessity to get a kid to eat something that, for some reason, will not be consumed if God forbid all these ingredients they love are mixed together.

I won't make a separate meal for a toddler because, frankly, I don't have time for that. But I have discovered that a plate of say, separated ground beef, onions, peppers, cheese and tortillas has a better chance of getting eaten than anything remotely resembling a taco. My poor children will never be as suave as the kid who can munch Mexican while playing Parkour, but at least they'll be nourished.

I've also found that kids tend to eat more if they're incorporated into the cooking process, at least for as long as their attention span allows.

"GET ME MY TWO-STEP! [Step-stool]" Chloe cried one day.

"What do you say?" I asked.

"Please."

"Put it in a sentence."

"Please may you get me my two-step."

"Thanks for your permission. Oh whatever — here. I've set it up for you."

Chloe climbed up on the step and surveyed the situation.

"Can I get some salt and pepper?"

"*Hey Yeah, I want to shoop baby... shoop, shoop bay doop...*" I sang.

"Huh?"

"One day you'll appreciate Salt-N-Pepa."

"What?"

"Never mind, here you can add salt and pepper."

When she was done with the pepper grinder, she pointed to the chicken.

"What is that?"

"Oooh don't touch that, it's raw meat," I said. "But that's a good question. See how it's pink? Poultry comes from chickens. Pork comes from pigs. And beef comes from cows."

"Cows come from Cowafornia."

"No, actually... well, there's a certain logic to it."

"This is the grossest dinner ever."

"It's chicken pot pie. PIE."

"Yeah, but it has vegetables."

"The vegetables are drowned in cream, topped by a pie crust... ugh never mind," I said and sighed.

I stuck dinner in the oven and about 20 minutes later Chloe came rushing around the corner.

"I SMELL PIE!" she said.

"Yes, again, that's dinner."

"I want some now! This is the best dinner ever!"

The girls actually ate a bit of dinner, too, before messing around, their new after-dinner routine.

"She showed me the food in her mouth!" Chetta shrieked.

"She tattled on me!" Chloe retorted.

"So," I said, trying to piece this all together. "You're tattling on her tattling on you?"

"Um..." Chloe said. "Yes."

Chapter 34: Chetta's Preschool

Shortly after Concetta started preschool, we bought her an alarm clock. It had a large green digital display with oversized buttons, and I explained to her how the "snooze" and "reset" buttons worked. She seemed to understand it well enough, though all that night I fretted about her first day waking up to an alarm. Would she figure it out? Would she get scared and cry?

As it turns out she did neither. I walked upstairs the next day and the clock was blaring next to her, announcing the start to a new day. Concetta was right next to it, still completely passed out. And here, everyone has been saying she doesn't take after me.

Since she's still 3, she's in half-day Pre-K, and I enjoy our lunches together mostly because I get to hear all the preschool gossip.

"So what did you learn today?" I said one day, as we were settling in for a gourmet lunch of deconstructed ham and cheese sandwich.

"I don't know," she said.

"What did you have for snack?" I asked.

"We had goldfish!" she announced, excited.

"And I was line leader!" she added, her pre-school drawl turning the honor into "wine weeder." Then her mood darkened. "But two kids CUT IN FRONT OF ME!"

"Oh no!" I said, aghast.

"Yeah," she went on, the tone of her voice escalating, as if she had just said, "*I walked around the corner. AND THEN I WITNESSED A MURDER!"* She looked at me gravely. "And Susie said a BAD WORD!"

"What was the... whoop never mind, I don't think I want to ask that. Oh dear. Well, did you read any books today?"

"Yes!" Chetta said, now clearly distraught. "We read a book about a zebra today and the zebra in the story had a shirt on but NO PANTS."

"No way," I said, trying to suppress a smile.

Chapter 35: Parenting in the Super Mario Age

One day in early adolescence I remember sitting at my house and my grandmother came in and sat on the couch behind me. After about 10 minutes or so of watching the TV, she told me, "This channel is broken. It keeps repeating itself. We have to reset it or something."

Sadly for me, I had to explain to her that actually the TV was fine. We weren't watching a channel at all. I was playing a level of Crash Bandicoot that was rather hard, which is why I kept dying. Also, I was pretty terrible. So there's that.

I've noticed that parenting has "leveled up" in the past several years because, in addition to making all the usual decisions about school, play and activities, now there's the balancing act of determining the right amount of media.

"No Internet" is too restrictive, obviously, because the Internet is a great way to research things quickly and interact with friends. On the other hand, you know there are the Rep. Anthony Weiners of the world who are going around sending girls pictures of their — you know, I still can't get over the fact his name was actually "Weiner."

Though, in some ways, of course, technology has made parenting much easier. I've found an audiobook makes cleaning up after your little one go much faster. And yes, sometimes the paper towels end up in refrigerator because you get a little distracted, but whatever.

Also, I think I've designed an app that will replace parents entirely. In lieu of exasperating yourself, you can just press one of the following buttons and your phone will shout:

1. *"SHHH!"*
2. *"WAIT! WASH YOUR HANDS!"*
3. *"CLOSE THE DOOR, YOU'RE LETTING ALL THE BUGS IN!"*
4. *"Say PLEASE"*
5. *"I'll tell you one more time: NO."* Or the infamous:
6. *"Because I SAID so."*

Once I asked Chloe to clean the living room. She balked and said she wanted to still play her video game. I asked her again and she kept whining that she didn't want to do it. Here is the irony, though: she was playing "Grandma's Kitchen." How could a game that features fun activities like "do the dishes" be more fun than actually cleaning up?

THEN I GOT AN IDEA.

I gathered the kids around.

"We are going to play a FUN new game," I told them. I took out a blank piece of paper and wrote some chores on it, with blank boxes next to each line.

"Every time you complete a task, you get a gold coin," I said, drawing a yellow dot in one of the blank boxes.

"Really?" Chloe said.

"Really. Okay, now the first part is picking up that puzzle..."

Chloe and Chetta fought over earning gold coins. Thank you, Super Mario Brothers, for teaching me parenting skills.

Chapter 36: Raising Football fans

Hubby is mostly a college football fan, though he also cheers for the Bengals whereas I cheer for the Eagles, and we are raising our children to be Beagles fans which is working out about as well as you'd think it wouldn't. However, the actual team doesn't matter as much to the girls because my two little charmers have figured out they can stretch bedtime by saying the magic word to daddy – football.

When the Bengals played the Eagles I asked, "Who are you rooting for, Chetta?

"The Bengals!" she shouted. I was exasperated.

"Do you know what a Bengal is?"

"They cheat."

"What?"

"They cheat."

"Oh, is this because they look like cheetahs?"

"Yeah."

"Oh, honey," I said. "Cheetahs don't actually cheat, that's just their name."

"What?"

Chapter 37: Getting Dressed

The other day I yelled up to Chetta, "Get changed!"

"Okay!" she yelled back, and I heard scurrying around her room.

Ten minutes later I went upstairs and she wasn't in her room. I heard water running. I went into the bathroom where she was perched on the side of the sink, in the same clothes as before. Her foot was in the sink, under the tap. Oh, and it was bright orange.

"What are you doing?!" I shrieked.

"I'm... getting changed?" she tried.

Getting dressed is, for little girls, the ultimate in self-expression and, thankfully, early on they insist on assembling their own on outfits. Chloe threw a fit the other day when I wouldn't let her wear the same clothes from the day before. Don't get me wrong, "Batgirl" is the ultimate in underwear awesomeness, but even superheroes should have some hygienic standards.

Chetta also has a favorite set of clothes that she insists on wearing every time she gets them back from the wash: her Queen Elsa getup. Which features long snowflake pants and fur on the long-sleeve shirt. Did I mention it's 102 degrees here in the summer?

At the same time, getting dressed requires a dedication to following through on many steps, which can be quite a challenge when you have the attention span of a squirrel. I'm amazed how someone can assiduously steal mommy's makeup and spend hours properly painting your eyelids the right shade of blue, yet often get distracted after putting on underwear and not have a problem running around the house half-naked.

A few months ago, I took them to the gym for swim lessons because, as we've established, there can never be too much mommy hot tub time. Both girls had chosen their own swimsuits for the occasion, and I helped Concetta out of the car because she is still too small to unbuckle her car seat.

She hopped cheerily out of the car but I froze as she skipped onto the sidewalk and I caught a full moon. Having dressed herself, she had put the top to her tankini on correctly, but on her bottom she put ... another swimsuit top. *Oh, oh, oh my God. My kid is wearing assless chaps,* I thought, trying not to panic. *In public.*

I ran over and scooped her up quickly.

"What's wrong?" she said, as I scooted an arm below her bare bum.

"Oh, nothing," I said, nonchalant. "You know what? Your sister has swim lessons first, and then I think you are going to wear her suit today, to try it out."

"Really?" she said, eyes wide. Chloe rarely shares clothes with her sister until she outgrows them.

"Yes, just for today," I said.

Chapter 38: Christmas

For our very first Christmas with Chloe, we went to my parents' house. While my mom was out getting food, the dog, Max, started barking. I texted her, but my phone decided to auto-correct "fed" as "f'ed." So my text message turned into, "Doesn't the dog usually get f'ed at 4?"

Max was an extremely old dog, though, and thanks to being completely senile, he did not really care when he was getting slapped by an overzealous baby, unlike our cats who don't like it at all. Chloe was in heaven.

As a kid, I thought, *The Christmas season is SO long. How will I ever wait until Christmas?* As an adult I think, t*he Christmas season is SO short. How will I ever get all this crap done before Christmas?* Seriously, how is it that in Victorian England they had time to chop all their firewood, wash all their dishes manually, wash all their clothes via scrub tub, go everywhere on foot, and yet they still found time to write out all Christmas cards by hand, bake all Christmas treats from scratch and deck the halls with boughs of holly?

This past Christmas, I was up one night for quite a long time wrapping things after the girls finally went to bed. I had wrapping paper, scissors, gift tags and presents scattered all over the living room floor. I was moving between each present by walking around on my hands and knees trying to cover everything as efficiently as possible. Unfortunately, I didn't realize the scissors were behind me when I moved back and inadvertently stabbed myself. To the point of bleeding. THROUGH my jeans.

I thought about going to the ER to get some stitches, but then how exactly would that go down?

Doctor: Oh, my gosh. What happened here?

Me: Yes, you see I had a very intense crafting accident...

Doc: A CRAFTING accident?

Me: Yes, bear with me here...

So I have a little scar now on my left knee. I thought about posting a picture of it on the Internet to enhance my street cred, but then I figured that would blow up when people figured out I wasn't actually a "hard core rapper" but rather a "hard core wrapper."

We went again to my parents' house this Christmas. When we got to the airport, Chloe was upset that we were boarding with the families because she, of course, wanted to board with the "C" group.

When we got on the plane, Chetta asked, "Why are all these people going to Nona's house?"

Finally, on Christmas morning, Chloe and Chetta came downstairs and gazed in wonderment at all the things that Santa left behind. And, I should say, wrapped expertly.

Each opened a few presents. Chetta started obsessing over new coloring books and Chloe was trying to open Mouse Trap.

"Want to open the rest of your presents?" my dad asked.

"No, thank you," Chloe said sweetly.

Chapter 39: Children's Art

"Mommy, I made you a picture!" Chloe gleefully shouted one day.

"Oh, is this a frog?" I said.

"No, it's you silly!" Burn.

"Oh, I see," I said.

"I peeked from upstairs so I could get it just right," she continued.

"That's just a wonderful likeness," I agreed. Mmm. Yeah.

I didn't want to be that mom who

throws out their kids' drawings. Which is why I recycle them.

I do keep a few of the best, of course, but if I kept every single piece, or the majority of them even, our house might be featured on an episode of *Hoarders*. For children, I find art is a confusing prospect. There are so many rules: Color in the lines. Don't yell at your sister for coloring the "wrong" color. Don't color on the wall. Don't color your face. It is one of the few activities though, where kids can really express themselves, which is why I think it's so important.

"Mom, I made you this picture!" Chloe shouted the other day. It was a series of colored dots scattered across a white sheet of paper.

"Thanks honey, it's beautiful," I said, taking it to look at it.

"Uh no, it goes this way," she said, turning the page.

"Oh yeah, of course," I said, as if this were obvious. I hesitated for a minute. "Uh, so what is it?" I finally said.

"It's art!"

"Oh, of course."

Chapter 40: Working Parent

Unfortunately, my office is always terribly cold. The sad part is I work from home.

In general, I love having a home office. I know that some people dread having their email follow them everywhere, but I think it's much better than being tethered to a desktop somewhere at the end of a long commute. Plus, I'd much rather take my kids and some legal paperwork to the park and enjoy some sunshine at the same time.

"Here mom!" Chetta said one day, while I wasn't really paying attention.

"Ok, thanks," I said, lost in whatever I was reading. Finally, I looked down. "GAH!" I screamed.

"It's a dead bug." Chetta said.

"Yah," I replied.

You know you're particularly rocking this mom thing when your kid interrupts "Horton Hears a Who" because she has to take a call from "Jim," her "friend from work," on her "cell."

For some reason, though, tiny people seem to get overly jealous whenever I am on the phone. I ask my kids to clean up and mysteriously they vanish. I get on the phone for a minute and they appear out of nowhere. And yes, I have asked them to clean up first in the hopes that I can take a call, only to witness them apparate out of the woodwork and loudly announce their presence.

Also, my work desk is the most interesting toy box in the house. For the same reason that the most efficient way to dress a toddler is to, in fact, dress her panda and tell her she can't wear those clothes, the desk is tempting as the forbidden fruit. It has tape, scissors, paper and a plethora of fun things attractive to the crafting set. Bonus points if you discover some sharp push pins and accidentally leave some on Mommy's seat.

Once, in a pre-coffee haze, I sat down at my computer to do work only to discover that moving the mouse left made the cursor move right and vice versa. *AHHH this thing is broken*, I panicked. Of course, after a minute, I realized that the mouse was fine, it had just been sabotaged. *You idiot, it's upside down.*

The other day my phone rang.

"Hello?" I said.

"Yes hi, this is [So-and-So], you had left a message with our office?" the caller said.

"Oh, yes of course," I said, rummaging around for a pen.

"I have the phone number for [Source] that you were looking for," she said.

"Ok great, thank you so much," I said, now frantically scouring my desk drawer. I found two compasses, six unsharpened pencils and one pink "Beauty and the Beast" marker.

"The number is-"

"Ooh, sorry hold on a second, let me just find a pen," I said.

"Okay," said the caller, a trifle annoyed.

I spied a crayon wrapper hidden under a stack of papers on one side. *Well this isn't ideal, but whatever I'm sure it will work...*

"Go ahead," I said confidently.

The caller started the number again as I tried to write it down. *ARGH! OF COURSE it's a white crayon.*

Chapter 41: Baby Brudder

To the delight of Chloe and Chetta, a new member of the family will be joining us soon. My own brother was born when I was 6 and it was like getting a baby doll for Christmas. Not just a talking doll or a feeding doll, but one who did everything! I could even change his little diaper, which was so much fun. Does everybody hear me? It was incredibly fun, please enforce this concept with my girls.

Being pregnant is a little easier the third time around because you know what to expect. Namely, that all body parts will crap out on you.

One morning I was feeling kind of down on myself because I was tired, I had a cold and I was drinking more fluids with a bowling ball on my bladder — not fun.

Then I felt the urge to sneeze.

And realized I was holding a full cup of coffee.

So, yes, if you can imagine a hippo attempting ballet while spinning cups on a rubber ball, that was me as I tried to put down the mug gently and run for the bathroom. Instead I sneezed, peed my pants and spilled some of the coffee.

Freewheel fail.

Chetta has told me she will be the

"medium sister," which I suppose makes more sense than "middle child" anyway. She seems overly amazed at the very prospect of the baby. The other day, when I was wearing a tight shirt, she ran up to my belly and squealed.

"OH MY GOSH!" she shrieked. "I FOUND THE BABY'S EYE!"

"No, honey," I said, "that's just my belly button."

Unfortunately, though, 3-year-olds have no sense of time and she has been asking me nonstop when the baby will arrive.

"Not for several more months." I said one day. "He's got a lot more cooking to do."

Concetta looked at me in horror.

"You can't COOK the baby!" she replied.

Chloe is also jazzed to be the "biggest sister" and is getting dangerously close to figuring out this whole baby thing.

"When I get big, I can pick out a husband!" she said to me one day.

"Whoa, ho. Okay." I stammered. "I'm not even cool with dating yet. Hey, you know what would be fun? You could be a nun!"

"And I can have children!"

"So... are we totally past the nun idea? I think we've established that would be fun."

"Don't worry mom, I'll let you hold one."

"That's very generous," I said.

She sighed. "I can't wait to have kids."

"Don't rush it."

"OK, if I don't want to have kids, I'll cut my hair real short."

"It doesn't work like that."

"How does it work?"

"Um..." I hesitated.

She looked puzzled, as if putting something together.

"But wait how do you know there's a baby IN your tummy?"

"That's a good question. There are a lot of ways and some are a little too complicated to explain now, but mostly I know because I want to throw up all the time," I said.

"Oh," she said.

She got out the baby names book and started writing down a list of her favorites for us to choose from: Cici and Rainbow, of course. Cowboy or "CB" for short. Nemo because we had just seen "Finding Dory."

Shortly afterward, I put them to bed. I finished up "Green Eggs and Ham" and tried to tuck them in for the night.

"That book was for the baby," Chetta said.

"Aw that's so sweet. I'm sure he enjoyed it, too," I said.

"I get another book," she explained. "For me."

Conclusion

It's a typical night in our household. We come in from playing. I tell Chloe, "I don't know how long we'll last in this heat."

"What does last mean?" she asked.

"Well, it can mean a lot of things," I said. "But in this case it's how long we can endure. Do you know what endure means?"

"Yup," she said confidently. "It means you're inside."

I start to make dinner. Concetta complains because she wants Cheetos for dinner. I explain that Cheetos are not good for you, so you can't eat them all the time.

"But I don't want to eat them all the time, I just want to eat them for dinner," she points out. I again tell her no.

She pouts and walks away and goes to get sympathy from Daddy who is watching SportsCenter. I overhear her and start to think perhaps she only partly understood my discussion regarding the triceratops' roar button. She explains to him, "This is where the annoying comes out. When you press this button."

We have dinner and all talk about our days and how they went and what we did.

Then we all go up for bath time. Chloe has a problem trying to get her foam toys to adhere to the bathtub.

"This doesn't stick good!" she wails.

So I help her out.

"This doesn't stick WELL," I say.

Later we all read stories and while reading Snow White, Chloe asks, "Why is that dwarf 'Sleepy?'"

And I tell her the obvious answer: "He probably has little kids."

Then I send them both to bed.

It's funny. If you got into a terrible car accident that took you six weeks to recover, no one would expect you to water a cactus regularly, let alone give you a human being in need of round-the-clock care. Yet this is exactly what happens to women who give birth. Most eventually repeat the process.

I had a revelation one night, while balancing a bottle of milk in one hand and a glass of wine in another, that I will probably never win the mother of the year award. But then, I will never be a helicopter parent either and I hear those are really bad.

The point is, has anyone literally applauded one of your accomplishments today? Say, because you successfully used the potty? Did anyone offer to get you toilet paper and even wad it up for you? No? Then you need a kid.

And yes, perhaps your kid too will grow up to be a smartass. But then what a terrible place the world would be if we were all so serious about ourselves.

The other day, Hubby and I were each holding one of Chloe's hands and she was shouting, "One, two, three, weeee!" Then we lifted her up.

"One, two, three, weeee!" she shouted again, and again we lifted her up.

"Okay," Hubby said. "Now let's count to five."

"One, two, five!" she shrieked and then jumped with all her might.

Acknowledgements

First, I would like to thank my family for their enduring love and support, despite having to put up with a smartass like me.

Second, I'd like to thank my lovely editor, Laura Gaton, who is twice the mother I am. No, seriously people, she has twins. BOYS. Someone edit this to make it sound more dramatic.

Third, I'd like to thank Pronoun Books for publishing this and helping authors everywhere.

Last, I'd like to thank our neighbors, all the people in our church, the people at our kids' school, and all the friends we have made in Oklahoma and beyond. We are blessed to have you in our lives and thank you for listening to our insufferable stories.

CPSIA information can be obtained at www.ICGtesting.com
Printed in the USA
BVOW06s2340200916

462753BV00021BA/128/P